Twayne's English Authors Series

Sylvia E. Bowman, *Editor*

INDIANA UNIVERSITY

Michael Drayton

(TEAS) 52

Michael Drayton

By Joseph A. Berthelot
United States Air Force Academy

Twayne Publishers, Inc.   ::   New York

CUM AMORE AD MATREM MEAM

"Only that little which to me was lent,
I give thee back, when all the rest is spent."

Preface

This study of Michael Drayton traces his literary development over a forty-year period. From a relatively second-rate Petrarchist in his early years, he became a highly diversified and accomplished, if not great, poet in his later days. In the six major editions of his sonnet sequence he began with the highly stylized conventions used by such Petrarchists as Sir Philip Sidney and Samuel Daniel. In the early sonnets Drayton's poetic view was almost completely circumscribed by a view of an artificial world. By the time he published his third revised edition in 1600, he was beginning to discard many of the flamboyant conventions he had used earlier; he began to write sonnets which depicted a realistic view of life in a very dramatic manner.

In his pastorals he started with a work which was strongly influenced by Edmund Spenser's *Shepherds Calendar.* However, he omitted his master's satiric views, remaining content to comment on the state of poetry and to lament the passage of the Golden Age. More than any of his contemporaries Drayton used his pastorals as a vehicle for escape literature rather than as a setting for a serious comment on some aspect of life. In his later pastorals he outgrew the strong influence of Spenser with the result that the works came closer to the Classical vein of the Theocritan idylls. Finally, in *The Muses Elizium,* he created a highly idealized pastoral setting which contained the distillation of his best previous experiments in this mode. In his constant revisions and later pastorals Drayton utilized the same principles he had used to compose his later sonnets. He dropped the superfluous decorations and attempted to achieve, with some success, a lyric simplicity.

With the exception of *Englands Heroicall Epistles* his historical poetry does not exhibit the best of his poetic talents, although much of it will amply repay the reader's interest. However, in the revisions and rewritings of his legends and *Mortimeriados* the same change is noted in rhetoric and syntax apparent in the reworking of his sonnets and pastorals.

Poly-Olbion is an unusual work combining the topographical, historical, mythological, and other patriotic elements which glorified England. Because of its immense length of almost fifteen thousand lines, Drayton did no rewriting after its first publication. However, in it he utilized the experience he had gained in his writing of the pastoral and historical poems. This topographical work best exemplifies his middle period in which he escaped the restrictions of the formal Petrarchist conventions but had not yet achieved the direct simplicity of his later poetry.

Drayton's lyrics especially portray his poetic development in the last half of his literary career. Several odes reflect the styles and attitudes of the Cavalier or Metaphysical schools of poetry. In his odes he avoided the flamboyancies of his early Petrarchan period and achieved either the light cynicism of the Cavalier poets in "The Rivall" or the nervous perspective of the Metaphysicals in "The Heart" and "The Cryer." In "The Ballad of Agincourt" he triumphantly managed a tight compression of the patriotic and militant spirit which had dully motivated his long historical poems. Also in his Horatian epistles, which he termed elegies, he wrote in a strong, virile style similar to that of Ben Jonson.

Drayton's early expressed views on the nature of poetry and poets were completely in accord with the ideas held by the English Petrarchists. He was also greatly influenced by Guillaume DuBartas' Neoplatonic notions. To them poetry was the "divine science," and poets were the anointed priesthood. However, in the second half of his career he discarded his artificial views and attempted to describe reality in his works. This change in his world view resulted in poetry which was vital and dynamic.

These general comments on Drayton should clearly indicate the specific aims of this book. First of all, I want to present him as the complete Renaissance poet, one who wrote effectively in almost all of the poetical forms of his day—a sonneteer, a lyricist, a pastoralist, an historical and topographical poet. One of my contentions is that the whole Drayton canon gives a reader a meaningful representation of most of the poetic material, modes, and styles popular from 1590 to 1630. Since another major purpose of this work is to illustrate how Drayton evolved in style, thought, and perspective, I intend to place special emphasis on the analysis of his sonnet sequence. Although he was an in-

Preface

veterate reviser, he outdid himself in revising and reissuing this sequence. From 1593 when *Ideas Mirrour* first appeared, he revised and rewrote, added and deleted again and again. Therefore in the first chapter I take special pains to trace his growth as a poet through the six major editions of *Idea*. After investigating the sonnets thoroughly, the reader should then be able to discern how changes occur in the many other genres in which Drayton composed.

Because of the specific scope of this book there are some facets only lightly touched upon. For instance, minimal attention is paid to a discussion of the specific source materials which Drayton used and also to a comparison of his contemporaries' work in the same genre as Drayton's. Extensive analysis of these important literary aspects is not, I feel, appropriate to my basic purposes. Both of these are comprehensively covered in the studies of Glen P. Haskell, Ray L. Heffner, Jr., Vernam E. Hull, and William Wiatt. But then each of these scholars was working with much smaller segments of Drayton's poetry than this view of his entire canon.

I wish to express my thanks to Dr. Harold Priest of Denver University who advised me so kindly and so often and also to Dr. Cortland Pell Auser of the City College of New York for his able reading of the draft and for his valuable suggestions. For bearing with me during the long period I have worked at this task, I owe a special debt of gratitude to Eva M. Berthelot, my mother.

JOSEPH ALFRED BERTHELOT

United States Air Force Academy
March, 1966

Contents

Chronology

1563   Michael Drayton born at Hartshill, North Warwickshire.

1591   *The Harmony of the Church* published; confiscated and burned by orders of the church officials at Lambeth.

1593   *Idea, The Shepheards Garland* appeared, also *Piers Gaveston, Earl of Cornwall.*

1594   *Ideas Mirrour*, the first edition of the sonnet sequence, and *Matilda* published.

1595   *Endimion and Phoebe, Ideas Latmus* printed.

1596   *Mortimeriados* and *The Tragical Legend of Robert, Duke of Normandy.* The latter contained revised and shortened versions of *Gaveston* and *Matilda.*

1597   *Englands Heroicall Epistles.* Also for the next five years Drayton worked for Philip Henslowe writing for the theater in collaboration variously with Anthony Mundy, Thomas Dekker, John Webster, Henry Chettle, Robert Wilson, and Thomas Middleton.

1598   Five more epistles added to *Englands Heroicall Epistles.*

1599   *Idea*, the first major revision of his sonnet sequence, appeared, one more epistle added to his collection, and his only extant play, *The First Part of the True and Honorable Historie of the Life of Sir John Old-Castle, the good Lord Cobham*, produced.

1603   *Mortimeriados* rewritten under the name of *The Barons Warres*; also *To the Majestie of King James.*

1604   *The Owle* published, *A Paean Triumphall* in honor of the new king, and *Moyses in a Map of His Miracles* also printed.

1605   *Poems* consisted of revised versions of *The Barons Warres*, the *Epistles*, and the three legends written thus far.

1606   *Poems Lyrick and Pastorall* contained *Eclogs* (a complete revision of *The Shepheards Garland*), *The Man in the Moon* (a rewriting of *Endimion and Phoebe*), and twelve *Odes.*

1607   *The Legend of the Great Cromwell*, the last of Drayton's four legends, published.

1608 *Poems*, a reprinting of the 1605 edition with a slightly revised version of *Idea*, the sonnet sequence.

1610 *Poems* of 1608 reissued.

1612 *Poly-Olbion*, containing only the first eighteen songs with a learned commentary by Selden.

1613 *Poems* of 1610 reprinted.

1618 Published two elegies in *Certain Elegies, done by sundrie Excellent Wits*.

1619 *Poems*, a major revision containing all of his earlier poetry except *Poly-Olbion* with eight new odes added.

1622 Reprinted the first eighteen songs of *Poly-Olbion* and added the newly written last twelve songs.

1627 *The Battaile of Agincourt* also contained many new major poems—*The Miseries of Queene Margarite, Nymphidia, The Quest of Cynthia, The Shepheards Sirena, The Mooncalfe,* and twelve elegies.

1630 *Poems* basically a reprint of the 1619 edition, and his final work *The Muses Elizium* with *Noahs Floud, David and Goliah,* and *Moses His Birth and Miracles,* a rewriting of the 1604 Moses poem.

1631 Died about 23 December and was buried in the north aisle of Westminster Abbey.

Aside from his publications little pertinent information is known about his life. He served in his early years the Sir Henry Goodere family. From 1590 on Drayton lived in London and worked on his poetry. He was friend of almost every important literary figure from then until his death.

Michael Drayton

CHAPTER 1

The Sonnet Sequence

THE glory that was Spain had been rotting on the bottom of the English Channel for six long years, and the glory that was England had reached its zenith in this the beginning of the last and most brilliant decade of Elizabeth's reign. *The Faerie Queene* had made her first entrance upon the scene, and the young Shakespeare had won acclaim with his *Venus and Adonis*. In this year of 1594 the young poet, Michael Drayton, known to all for his pastoral, *Idea, the Shepheards Garland*, gave an eager audience his new sonnet sequence, *Ideas Mirrour*.

The sonnet sequence, with which Drayton was to work so long and so fruitfully, came to England from Italy by way of France in 1582 with the publication of Thomas Watson's *Hekatompathia*. Nine years later the genre surged toward popularity with the posthumous edition of Sir Philip Sidney's *Astrophel and Stella*. From this point on for the next ten years almost every important poet wrote and issued his own attempt in this new genre.[1] After the death of Queen Elizabeth, however, this type of poetic collection quickly faded from the public view.

When Michael Drayton published the first edition of his sonnet sequence, *Ideas Mirrour, Amours in Quatorzains*, the popularity of this genre was approaching its high point. However, unlike many of the other sonneteers, Drayton continued to work in this form long after the general public interest in it had waned. He made his first major revision in 1599, and followed this with further revisions in 1600, 1602, 1605, and 1619. It is the study of the differences in these editions—the sonnets dropped, rewritten, revised, and added—which aids the student in an analysis of Drayton's growth as a poet.

The very title of the sequence, *Ideas Mirrour, Amours in Quatorzains*, which he changed to *Idea* for the 1599 and subsequent editions, is significant. The use of *Amours* or "loves" to designate the sonnets reflects the influence of Pierre de Ronsard and Joachim DuBellay. And the basic title, which seems to have come from Claude de Pontaux who had published a sequence *L'Idee* in 1579, refers also to the platonic idea of beauty as used by members of the Pleiade. *Idea* was an imaginative address to beauty as represented by the river Ankor in the same way as Petrarch had written of the Po and the Rhone, Sidney of the Thames, and Samuel Daniel of the Avon. The most recent critics extended this notion further. They suggested that just as the Rhone was equated with Laura to Petrarch, the Thames with Stella to Sidney, and the Avon with Delia to Daniel, so the Ankor represented a real woman, here named Idea, to Drayton.

The general consensus of critics is that Anne Goodere was the Idea of Drayton's poetry. Drayton spent many years in service to the Goodere family at Poleworth, and continued his interest in the family throughout his life even when he lived in London. In fact, many of the critics argue whether or not a strong personal passion was involved in his poetic inspiration for the sonnets to Idea. However, to anyone familiar with the poetic techniques of the English Renaissance, it seems obvious that Drayton was following the dictates of convention and friendship and not personal love in choosing Idea, Anne Goodere, as the object of his sonnet sequence. The majority of the sonnets which carry the heaviest strain of passionate love are written almost completely in the most rhetorical Petrarchan manner. An analysis of the entire one hundred and six sonnets shows much too broad a spectrum in subject matter and in techniques for the sequence to be classified as one "hammered in the white heat of love" reflecting impassioned "fits of despair and gleams of hope."[2] The best way to determine Drayton's motivation is to look at each of the editions to see how his ideas and methods changed over the twenty-five-year period from the first edition to the last major revision.

I Ideas Mirrour, Amours in Quatorzains (*1594*)

Drayton's first offering to the public of his sonnet sequence was not remarkably different from the other sonnet sequences of the same period. A study of the fifty-two sonnets of this edition shows many of the same techniques, images, and ideas which had started with Petrarch and continued through the French Amours of Ronsard, Desportes, and de Pontaux to the English sonnets of Wyatt, Watson, Sidney, and Daniel. In fact, Sir Sidney Lee asserts that Drayton borrowed everything in his sonnets from either his predecessors or his contemporaries.[3] Other critics are not so harsh, admitting the similarity of themes and images, but maintaining that these were actually the common property of the Petrarchan sonneteer. Stopes says that the Drayton sonnets "openly imitate the sonnets of the French school, yet are undoubtedly based on personal experience."[4] Kathleen Tillotson, J. William Hebel, and Bernard Newdigate maintain that none of his sonnets are direct translations from either the French or the Italian, but that they do show a marked influence at times.[5] Leah Jonas adds that in specific sonnets we can clearly see the influence especially of Sidney and Daniel.[6]

Ideas Mirrour contains Drayton's earliest efforts in the sonnet form and is at times youthful and sentimental. In this last decade of Queen Elizabeth's reign the influence of the Petrarchists was at its height, and it was only natural for a young poet to utilize the accepted conventions and conceits. Thus Idea becomes a fair, chaste, virtuous, cruelly unresponsive mistress; and Drayton the poet becomes the faithful, chivalrous, idealistic, and devoted lover. For the most part we have these same strains repeated over and over again in sixteenth-century love poetry. They were indeed the sonneteers' stock-in-trade.

In the dedicatory sonnet Drayton tells us two very important things for our purposes:[7]

> Vouchsafe to grace these rude unpolish'd rymes,
>   Which long (deer friend) have slept in sable night,
>   And come abroad now in these glorious tymes,
>   Can hardly brook the pureness of the light.
> But sith you see their destiny is such,
>   That in the world their fortune they must try,
>   Perhaps they better shall abide the touch,
>   Wearing your name their gracious livery.
> Yet these mine own, I wrong not other men,
>   Nor traffic further then this happy Clime,
>   Nor filch from Portes nor from Petrarchs pen,
>   A fault too common in this latter time.
> Divine Sir Phillip, I avouch thy writ,
> I am no pickpurse of anothers wit.

In this lyric we learn that many of the poems in this edition had been written prior to 1594, and that Drayton was denying writing conscious imitations of other poets. Of course, in keeping with the idea of art at this point in history, it was perfectly proper and just for a poet to pick up someone else's work and then re-shape it, restyle it, and above all, improve it with a new inspiration. Sir Philip Sidney as one having Classical authority had himself given expression and approval to this practice in his *Defense of Poesy*. Thus, with this concept in mind, we cannot accuse a Renaissance poet of plagiarism or mere copying when we find similarities or close parallels in the works of other poets. To the Elizabethan reader the test of improvement on the original source was the key to these approved borrowings.

Thus we can easily understand Drayton's avowal of originality even though in the very first sonnet we see that the beginnings of "Read here, sweet maid, the story of my woe" seem to come from Daniel's "Read in my face a volume of despair." But, as Oliver Elton points out, Drayton's version rises far above a "servile pencil tracing" of Daniel's poem. Yet again in the same way Amour 7 "Thyselfe thus burned in this sacred flame" is close to *Delia* 3 "with thy sacred flame,/Consume my life," and in Amour 10 the bookkeeping image "cast the sum of all my cares" has an approximation in "cast the accounts of all my cares" in *Delia*.[8]

Many of the conceits which Drayton used are found in several other poets' works. So, when Drayton likened his love to a ship tossed on stormy seas in Amour 34, he used the same figure as Sir Thomas Wyatt's "My Galley charged with Forgetfulness," Lodge's *Phillis* 11, and Spenser's *Amoretti* 82. The notion in Amour 31, "Sitting alone, Love bids me go and write," of the poet writing at love's dictation was used by Sidney, and would reappear again in Shakespeare's Sonnet 84. As in many of early sonnets, he was using figures and conventions held in common by the Petrarchist poets.

The traditional debate between the eyes and the heart appears in Amour 33:

> Whilst thus mine eyes do surfet with delight,
>   My wofull hart imprisoned in my brest,
>   Wishing to be trans-formed into my sight,
>   To look on her by whom mine eyes are blest.
> But whilst mine eyes thus greedily do gaze,
>   Behold, their objects over-soon depart,
>   And treading in this never-ending maze,
>   Wish now to be transformed into my hart.

> My hart surcharg'd with thoughts, sighs in abundance raise,
>> My eyes made dim with looks, pour down a flood of tears,
>> And whilst my hart and eye, envy each others praise.
>> My dying looks and thoughts are pieced in equall fears.
> And thus whilst sighs and tears together do contend,
> Each one of these, doth aid unto the other lend.

This same argument was carried on in Henry Constable's *Diana*, "my heart. mine eye accuseth of his death," in Thomas Watson's *Tears of Fancie* 19, 20, and later in Shakespeare's "Mine eyes and heart are at a mortal war."[9]

In Amour 2 Drayton implied the starlike quality in the eyes of Idea in his last couplet: "Those eyes to my hart shining ever bright/When darknes hath obscur'd each other light." And in sonnet 65 (1600) he called her "Bright star of beauty." This glorifying the eyes of the mistress as stars was a very common Petrarchism. In *Fidessa* 39 Bartholomew Griffin wrote "Fidessa eyes brightest stars of heaven"; in *Chloris* 2 William Smith, "Bright crystal beam and starbright eyes of Chloris"; in *Parthenophil* 57 Barnaby Barnes, "graces like stars in the face of Parthenope," and in 95 he speaks of Sidney's Stella as a star. And again in Amour 29 Drayton used the same image in a long apostrophe in a not too felicitous way:

> O starr of starrs, fair Planet mildly moving
> O Lamp of vertue, sun-bright, ever shining,
> O mine eyes Comet, so admir'd by loving,
> O clearest day-starr, never more declining.

In Amours 4 and 6, to name only two out of innumerable instances, Drayton made the customary Petrarchan claim that his poetry would confer immortality upon his mistress. Even after he later dropped many of his Petrarchan habits, this was one concept he would cling to throughout his poetic life. Any reader of the Renaissance sonnet is aware that this was one of the most common themes in the lyric poetry. Thus we can find the same in *Licia* 50, *Diana*, *Delia* 33, 37, 39, 40, 53, and *Amoretti* 29, 69, and 75, and throughout Shakespeare's sonnets.[10]

The apostrophe to sleep was another of the common Elizabethan poetic usages. So Sidney wrote "Come sleep! O Sleep, the certain knot of peace" in *Astrophel* 39; Daniel, "Care-charmer

Sleep, son of the sable night" in *Delia* 49; Griffin, "Care-charmer
Sleep, sweet ease is restless miser" in *Fidessa* 15; Barnes, "Dark
night! Black image of my foul dispair" in *Parthenophil* 83; and
William Drummond of Hawthornden wrote "Sleep, Silence
Child, sweet father of soft rest."[11] In Amour 45 Drayton took up
the same theme with far better results than most of his contemporaries:

> Black pitchy Night, companion of my woe,
>   The Inn of care, the Nurse of dreary sorrow,
>   Why lengthnest thou thy darkest hours so,
>   Still to prolong my long time lookt-for tomorrow?
> Thou sable shadow, Image of dispair,
>   Portrait of hell, the airs black mourning weed,
>   Recorder of revenge, remembrancer of care,
>   The shadow and the veil of every sinfull deed.
> Death like to thee, so live thou still in death,
>   The grave of joy, prison of days delight,
>   Let heavens withdraw their sweet Ambrozian breath,
>   Nor Moon nor stars lend thee their shining light.
> For thou alone renew'st that old desire,
> Which still torments me in days burning fire.

Even as Petrarch compared Laura to the immortal Phoenix,
the Elizabethan sonneteers used the same metaphor to describe
their poetic mistresses. The Phoenix bathed in its own creative
fire appears in the poems of Sidney, Giles Fletcher the elder,
Thomas Lodge, Daniel, and Smith. In Amour 6 the same image
is cast in an extravagant comparison. Although this was certainly
not one of Drayton's better sonnets as expressed in this edition,
it is worth quoting in full as an example of the metrical irregularities which are frequently found in the 1594 edition. It is also
valuable in that it can be compared with the rewritten versions
from 1599 and 1619. In this way we can immediately see the tremendous improvement of which Drayton was capable when he
revised his early work:

Amour 6

> In one whole world is but one Phoenix found,
>   A Phoenix thou, this Phoenix then alone,
>   By thy rare plume thy kind is easily known,
>   With heavenly colours dyed, with natures wonder crown'd,

Heap thine own vertues seasoned by their sun,
　On heavenly top of thy divine desire:
　Then with thy beauty set the same on fire,
　So by thy death, thy life shall be begun.
Thy self thus burned in this sacred flame,
　With thine own sweetness all the heavens perfuming,
　And still increasing as thou art consuming,
　Shalt spring again from th'ashes of thy fame;
And mounting up, shalt to the heavens ascend,
So may'st thou live, past world, past fame, past end.

"To the Phoenix" Sonnet 18 (1599)

Within the compass of this spacious round
Amongst all birds the Phoenix is alone,
Which but by you could never have been known,
None like to that, none like to you is found,
Heap your own vertues seasoned by their sun,
On heavenly top of your divine desire;
Then with your beauty set the same on fire,
So by your death, your life shall be begun.
Your self thus burned in this sacred flame,
With your own sweetness all the heavens perfuming
And still increasing as you are consuming,
Shall spring again from th'ashes of your fame,
　And mounting up, shalt to the heavens ascend,
　So may you live, past world, past fame, past end.

"An Allusion to the Phoenix" Sonnet 16 (1619)

'Mongst all the Creatures in this spacious Round,
Of the Birds kind, the Phoenix is alone,
Which best by you, of living Things is known;
None like to that, none like to you is found:
Your Beauty is hot and splend'rous Sun,
The precious Spices be chaste Desire,
Which being kindled by that heav'nly fire,
Your Life so like the Phoenix's begun;
Your self thus burned in this sacred flame,
With so rare sweetness all the Heav'ns perfuming,
Again increasing, as you are consuming,
Only by dying, born the very same:
　And wing'd by Fame, you to the Starrs ascend,
　So you of Time shall live beyond the End.

Another of the common techniques employed by the Petrarchans was the use of contrarieties. Sir Thomas Wyatt had long before set the example for English poets with his free translation of one of Petrarch's sonnets:

> I find no peace, and all my war is done;
> I fear and hope! I burn, and freeze like ice;
> I fly above the wind, yet can I not arise;
> And nought I have, and all the world I season. . . .

Barnes cried out in *Parthenophil* 31: "I burn yet am I cold! I am a cold, yet burn." Sidney concluded *Astrophel* 60 with "Blessed is my curse, and cursed is my bliss." And Spenser wrote in *Amoretti* 30: "My love is like to ice, and I to fire." Drayton used this same technique in Amour 32: "Those tears which quench my hope, still kindle my desire," and 50 "When first I ended, then I first began."

From these comparisons it is easy to see that Drayton was writing the same kind of sonnets as were his contemporaries. But it would be a mistake to maintain that he had no originality. Even in this first edition, which has so much in common with the other sonnet sequences of the day, there are many sonnets which prove that Drayton did possess an original and an inventive poetic fancy. Amour 30 has a strong and unusual metaphor:

> Three sorts of Serpents do resemble thee,
> That daungerous eye-killing Cockatrice,
> Th'inchaunting Syren, which doth so entice,
> The weeping Crocodile: these vile pernicious three.
> The Basilisk his nature takes from thee,
> Who for my life in secret wait do'st lie,
> And to my hart send'st poison from thine lie,
> Thus do I feel the pain, the cause, yet cannot see,
> Fair-maid no more, but Mermaid by thy name,
> Who with thy sweet alluring harmony
> Hast playd the thief, and stol'n my hart from me,
> And like a Tyrant mak'st my grief thy game.
> Thou Crocodile, who when thou hast me slain,
> Lament'st my death, with tears of thy disdain.

This sonnet is hardly the kind of lyric one would expect from a Petrarchan lover. The language is strong and forceful, and there seems to be a complete lack of playfulness. Yet the basic concept of the poem is directly from the Petrarchan convention in which the poet bemoans his grief at the treatment he receives from his mistress. It is primarily the comparison with the cockatrice, the siren, and the crocodile which seem to place it apart from the traditional lyric moan.

Another sonnet in which Drayton was working purely in the Petrarchan mode in a highly successful manner is Amour 25:

> The glorious sun went blushing to his bed,
>> When my souls sun came from her fair Cabinet,
>> Her golden beams had now discovered,
>> Lightning the world, eclipsed by his set.
> Some mus'd to see the earth deny the air,
>> Which from her lips exhal'd refined sweet,
>> A world to see, yet how he joy'd to hear
>> The dainty grass make music with her feet.
> But my most marvel was when from the skies,
>> So Comet-like each starr advaunc'd her light,
>> As though the heaven had now awak'd her eyes,
>> And summoned Angels to this blessed sight.
> No cloud was seen, but christaline the air,
> Laughing for joy upon my lovely fair.

This sonnet is so exquisitely Italianate in its lush rhetoric that it is worthy of Spenser's own hand. The concept within the lyric is hardly a profound one, but it has a strong beauty of its own. This beauty lies not in the idea of the poem but rather in the brilliant clothing of the image which gives the strength of emotion within the poem. This Amour has a rich texture comparing favorably with any of the other Petrarchan sonnets of the period.

Another excellent sonnet is Amour 26 "Cupid, dumb Idol, peevish Saint of Love." In it Drayton showed his impatience with the traditional symbol of love, Cupid, and supplanted him with a new goddess of love who is Idea herself. The second quatrain is especially good and has been so remarked by T. W. H. Crosland, Yvor Winters, and C. S. Lewis:

> Thy Bow half broke, is piec'd with old desire,
>> Her Bow is beauty, with ten thousand strings,
>> Of purest gold, tempred with vertues fire:
>> The least able to kill an host of Kings.

[25]

In 1594 Drayton was one of the chief wearers of Petrarch's mantle. Moreover, he generally retained the same spirit of worship at the shrine of love in the majority of his sonnets. He had taken the ideas, images, and techniques of his Petrarchan predecessors; and he had woven them into new sonnets, all his own.

The 1594 edition contained many metrical irregularities and variations in the rhyme schemes. For example, Amours 15 and 16 each has eighteen lines. And many of the Amours, as instanced by 7, 14, 17, 28, 30, 32, 33, and 10, contain hexameters. These departures from the accepted norm of a fourteen-line pentameter were to disappear gradually in the various revisions in later editions.

The critics are by no means in accord in their judgments of Drayton's first edition. Cyril Brett speaks of these first sonnets as "trials of skill" and "bubbles of the mind."[12] Kathleen Tillotson terms the substance of the works as synthetic with its use of old images of shipwreck (34), the wounded heart (6), planets (29, 47), the elements (27), disinterest and despair (37), with some new conceits as bookkeeping (10), the alphabet of love (11), and the use of the celestial numbers (8), which "illustrate the current straining after novelty."[13] Robert Hillyer suggests that Drayton was "so eager to pack everything into fourteen lines that the unyielding words burst with the pressure of such a mass of meaning." This pressure, although it damaged the technical qualities of the sonnets, added up to a "higher quality which transcends technique."[14] Lu Emily Pearson considers that the early sonnets were awkward because Drayton forced his conceits into predetermined molds. Drayton has his eye upon the picture he was drawing and not upon the lady, with the result that the 1594 Amours lacked the spontaneity of his later sonnets.[15]

Crosland believes that his early sonnets have evidences of originality in the "direct and vigorous strength of expression" which illustrated his love with "gusto and strength."[16] Lisle Cecil John holds that Drayton's weakness was in his choice of conceits. He condemns Drayton for "exaggerated personifications," "interjectional elaborateness," and "metaphoric apostrophes."[17] Of course, these very objections could be leveled against the entire body of Petrarchan conventions. Of the ten sonnets which John specifically singles out for objection, six were dropped in the first revision and the remainder greatly revised. C. S. Lewis writes "though Drayton can be human and heartfelt, still his imagery of voyage, phoenix, star, and river mediates beyond human passion. He is 'a Man that in some Trance, hath seene/ More than his wand'ring utt'rance can unfold,' one who 'builds his Hopes a world above the Skies.' "[18]

II Idea (*1599*)

The second sonnet sets the entire tone for the 1599 edition and helps to explain the major revisions and exclusions which Drayton had made in the sonnets of the first edition:

> Into these Loves, who but for Passion looks,
> At this first sight, here let him lay them by.
> And seek else-where, in turning others Books,
> Which better may his labour satisfy.
> No far-fetch'd Sigh shall ever wound my Brest,
> Love from mine Eye and a Tear shall never wring,
> Nor in Ah-mee's my whining Sonnets drest,
> (A Libertine) fantastickly I sing:
> My Verse is the true image of my Mind,
> Ever in motion, still desiring change;
> And as thus to Variety inclin'd,
> So in all Humours sportively I range:
>   My Muse is rightly of the English strain,
>   That cannot long one Fashion entertain.

In this new edition Drayton would no longer emphasize the traditional and conventional long-suffering vicissitudes of unrequited love. He would drop the "ah-mees" and replace them with a variety of moods and emotions. The sestet of the very next sonnet echoes this determination:

> My wanton verse nere keeps one certain stay,
> But now at hand; then seeks invention far,
> And with each little motion runs astray,
> Wild, madding, jocund and irregular;
>   Like me that lust, my honest mery rimes,
>   Nor care for Critic, nor regard the times.

These two sonnets indicate a definite and intended departure from many of the Petrarchan conventions which dominated his first edition. This new sequence of 1599 is not devoted to passion alone, but contains new themes and ideas.

For this edition Drayton dropped twenty-one of the earlier sonnets and added twenty-eight new ones.[19] Most of the excluded sonnets were heavy with bombastic conceits emphasizing adoration and love for Idea. A clear notion of the type of decorated sonnet which was dropped can be seen in the following: Amour 34, "My fayre, look from the turrets of thine eyes,/Into the ocean of a troubled mind"; Amour 23, "Wonder of Heaven, glass of divinitie,/Rare Beautie, Natures joy, Perfections Mother"; Amour 39, "Die, die my soul, and never taste of joy,/If sighes, nor tears, nor vows, nor prayers can move"; and Amour 40, "O thou unkindest fayre, most fayrest she,/In thine eyes triumph murdering my poor hart."

Amours 15 and 16 which had been cast into eighteen lines were dropped as part of his intention to regularize the metrics and form of the sonnets in the new edition. Then many of the lines in the retained sonnets written in alexandrines were redone into pentameter. So Amour 14 which had hexameter in lines 4, 8, and 14 was revised to obtain all pentameter lines. Amour 7 had a heptameter in line 14 and this was immediately replaced with a pentameter. Of the thirty-one Amours which were retained seventeen were revised in varying degrees in phraseology, rhyme, and rhythm. This variation in revision was from one or two words in some sonnets to a complete rewriting in the case of Sonnet 28. The other fourteen retained sonnets remained unchanged.

A comparison of Amour 32 with its revised form in 1599 as Sonnet 28 illustrates many of the things which Drayton was trying to accomplish in this edition:

Amour 32 (1594)

Those tears which quench my hope, still kindle my desire,
   Those sighs which cool my hart, are coals unto my love,
   Disdain Ice to my life, is to my soul a fire,
   With tears, sighs, and disdain, this contrary I prove.
Quenchless desire, makes hope burn, dries my tears,
   Love heats my hart, my hart-heat my sighs warmeth,
   With my souls fire, my life disdain out-wears,
   Desire, my love, my soul, my hope, hart and life charmeth.
My hope becomes a friend to me desire
   My hart imbraceth Love, Love doth imbrace my hart,
   My life a Phoenix is in my soules fire,
   From thence (they vow) they never will depart.

Desire, my love, my soul, my hope, my hart, my life,
With tears, sighs, and disdain, shall have immortal strife.

Sonnet 28 (1599) "To Contrarietie"

Those tears quench hope, do kindle my desire,
Those sighs cool harts, are coals unto my love,
Icy disdain, is to my soul a fire,
And yet all these I contrary do prove;
Desire doth make hope burn and dryeth tears,
Love heats my hart, which my sighs inly warmeth
With my souls gleed; disdain is spent to airs
It hurts and heals, it helpeth, and it harmeth.
My hope becomes a friend to my desire;
My hart imbraceth love, and love my hart.
Disdain a Phoenix is in my souls fire,
And vow from other, never to depart;
    Such peacefull conflicts stirring in my life,
    Foes live in concord, and friends still at strife.

First of all the new version regularizes the meter of the sonnet by changing the hexameter into pentameter. In the first version the lengthy line prevents the antitheses which operate in each line from being fully effective in building up the desired tension. The conflict which the poet sought never quite materialized. By shortening the line, the pressure upon the antitheses is forced to build up through the compression. By using more direct speech and dropping some of the relative pronouns, he made the conflict within the lines readily apparent to the ear and then to the emotions.

In his revision Drayton tried to achieve a greater coherence through use of a less complicated syntax. (This problem of trying to simplify a highly complicated syntax was one that plagued Drayton throughout his entire poetic career.) Although he was not completely successful, some lines from the revised edition can be compared with their earlier form to show what he attempted:

Sleeps wonder Beauty, wonders to worlds imparting,
Sleep watching Beauty, Beauty waking, sleep guarding,
       Amour 36 (1594) ll. 4-5

. . . .

> Either to other, miracles imparting
> Sleep watching Beauty, beauty soft sleep guarding.
>> Sonnet 16 (1599) ll. 4-5

The changes are relatively simple, but they do make the lines less complex and more effective:

> My hart surcharg'd with thoughts, sighs in abundance raise,
> My eyes made dim with looks, pour down a flood of tears,
> And whilst my hart and eye, envy each others praise,
> My dying looks and thoughts are piec'd in equal fears.
>> And thus whilst sighs and tears together do contend,
>> Each one of these, doth aid unto the other lend.
>>> Amour 33 (1594) ll. 9-14

> That Eyes had Heart, or that the Heart had Eyes,
> As covetous the others use to have:
> But finding reason still the same denies,
> This to each other mutually they crave;
>> That since each other they cannot be,
>> That Eyes could think, or that my Heart could see.
>>> Sonnet 33 (1599) ll. 9-14

In revising this passage Drayton not only removed some of the difficulties in the syntax, but he also removed many of the words and phrases which belonged to the love-sick sonneteer. Thus "sighes in abundance," "a flood of tears," "dying lookes," and "sighes and tears" disappear from the sonnet. The end result is a far better and more effective passage. The rhetoric has, in effect, become more closely balanced with the concept within the lyric.

Another method which Drayton used to achieve the mood he announced in Sonnets 2 and 3 was the careful arrangement of both the new and the old sonnets. He retained those sonnets from the 1594 edition which most closely harmonized with his desire for variety, and then placed them in alternate banks with the new ones. In the first fourteen sonnets only 4, 6, and 7 are from the 1594 edition and the rest are new. These retained sonnets were carefully chosen to avoid clashing with the new tone Drayton was seeking. Sonnets 15 through 20 are holdovers, and 21 through 25 are new. Those sonnets which were not in harmony with his spirit of laughter and variety, and which he thought too good to exclude, were placed near the end of the sequence where there would be no noticeable loss of effect. Therefore, the dedicatory sonnet and Amours 1, 2, 3, and 4 of 1594, the kind of lovesick sonnets he had disclaimed in Sonnet 2, became in 1599 sonnets 59, 49, 50, 51, and 52 respectively.

An additional technique which Drayton used to move the sequence away from the conventional amatory closeness to Idea was to include sonnets addressed to specific things, conditions, and mythological personages. He was able then to take some of the emphasis away from *Idea* by the addition of such titles as: 15, "To the Shadow"; 16, "To Sleep"; 18, "To the Phenix"; 20, "To the celestiall numbers"; 26, "To Despaire"; 28, "To Contrarietie"; 33, "To Imagination"; 35, "To Miracle"; 47, "An alusion to Dedalus and Icarus"; and 51, "An alusion to the Eglets"; and three of the new sonnets also received titles: 11, "To the Moon"; 23, "To the Sphears"; and 56, "A Cansonet."

The new lyrics in the 1599 edition clearly indicated Drayton's improvement as a sonneteer. For the past couple of years he had been engaged by Henslowe in writing drama with many of the most notable of the Elizabethan dramatists; therefore, it was not surprising that several of the new sonnets had a definite dramatic quality. This new attribute could easily be found in Sonnets 5, 8, 10, 12, 21, 24 (all of which were retained throughout the future revisions), and 27. Sonnet 5, "My Heart was slain, and none but you and I:/Who should I think the Murther to commit?" uses the common theme of the lover's heart being murdered by his cruel mistress: "Upon your Lips the scarlet drops are found,/And in your Eye, the Boy Cupid, or Love that did the Murther." However, in this case the argument is carried on in legal terms, using words like "verdict," "accessorie," and "evidence," with a resulting more serious tone than is customary with this theme. The dialogue is direct and dramatic, and the overall effect is more than pleasing.

The lover drinks wine made from his mistress's tears in Sonnet 10, "Love in a Humor, play'd the Prodigall,/And bad my Senses to a solemn Feast." Here the attitude is one of playfulness and of indifference to sentiment. Although the dramatic technique is good, the conceit is overstrained with the result—an unfortunate experiment.

Although frequently anthologized, Sonnet 8 is not one of his better dramatic sonnets. "Nothing but No and I, and I and No" is little more than a series of petulantly playful repetitions from the lover to Idea on the subject of her refusal to openly return his love. F. Y. St. Clair suggests that this sonnet together with 2, "Into these Loves, who but for Passion looks," 13, "You not alone, when You are still alone," and 14, "That learned father, which so firmly proves/The Soul of Man immortall and divine," is reminiscent of John Donne in the homeliness of the tone and language and in the metaphysical subtlety of 13. Yvor Winters also has high praise for 13.

Three of the dramatic sonnets in this edition are of very high quality. Sonnet 21 has a light airy tone. The lover takes the highly realistic point of view which he had promised us in Sonnet 2:

> You cannot love, my pretty Heart, and why?
> There was a time, You told me that you would,
> But now again You will the same deny,
> If it might please You, would to God, You could;
> What, will You hate? nay that You will not neither,
> Not love, nor Hate, how then? what will you do?
> What will you keep a mean then betwixt either?
> Or will you love Me, and yet hate me too?
> Yet serves not this: what next, what other Shift?
> You Will, and Will not, what a coil is here?
> I see your Craft, now I perceive Your Drift,
> And all this while, I was mistaken there:
> > Your love and Hate is this, I now do prove you,
> > You love in Hate, by Hate to make me love you.

Sonnet 24 has an old conceit, that of the exile of love from heaven, but with a completely new realistic approach:

> Love banish'd Heav'n, in Earth was held in scorn,
> Wand'ring abroad in Need and Beggary;
> And wanting Friends, though of a Goddess born,
> Yet crav'd the Alms of such as passed by:
> I, like a Man devout, and charitable,
> Clothed the Naked, lodg'd this wand'ring guest,
> With Sighs and Tears still furnishing his Table,
> With what might make the Miserable blest.
> But this ungrateful, for my good desert,

> Intic'd my Thoughts, against me to conspire,
> Who gave consent to steal away my Heart,
> And set my Brest, his Lodging, on a fire.
> > Well, well, my Friends, when Beggars grow thus bold,
> > No marvel then though Charity grow cold.

Sonnet 12 utilizes the inverted comparison. In the octet there is a description of a rich wastrel. In the third quatrain a metaphor is effectively applied to Idea's wasting of the love bestowed upon her, with the poet making a personal concluding comment in the couplet.

> To nothing fitter can I Thee compare,
> Then to the Son of some rich Penny-father,
> Who having now brought on his end with Care,
> Leaves to his Son all he had heap'd together;
> This new rich Novice, lavish of his chest,
> To one Man gives, and on another spends,
> Then here he riots, yet amongst the rest
> Haps to lend some to one true honest Friend.
> Thy gifts thou in Obscurity doest waste,
> False Friends thy kindness, born but to deceive Thee;
> Thy Love, that is on the unworthy plac'd,
> Time hath thy Beauty, which with Age will leave Thee;
> > Only that little which to Me was lent,
> > I give Thee back, when all the rest is spent.

Two of the sonnets of the 1599 edition have been suggested as having parallels in two Shakespearian sonnets. Sonnet 20, "An evill spirit haunts me still," has been compared to Shakespeare's 144, "Two loves have I of comfort and despair."[20] Both poets protest the corrupting influence of purely physical love alone. Drayton described specifically the evil of love in a woman who does not possess beauty of spirit, whereas, Shakespeare seemed to oppose this with the pure love of friendship. Drayton's 56, "Eyes with your tears, blind if you be,/Why have these tears such eyes to see," has been offered as a basic parallel to Shakespeare's 148, "O me, what eyes hath Love put into my head,/ Which have no correspondence with true sight!"[21] In the first case tears caused by love blind the eyes to reality, and in the other love itself makes the eyes see awry.

Another new element in this edition is the number of sonnets which comment either directly or indirectly upon Drayton's contemporary critics. Drayton carefully noted what the critics had to say, and at times he acted upon their advice. Thus after he made Idea a tenth Worthy in Amour 8, he read a biting epigram by Sir John Davies, addressed "In Decium." (Decius was Davies' name for Drayton.)

> Audacious painters have nine worthies made,
> But poet Decius more audacious far,
> Making his mistres march with men of war,
> With title of tenth worthy doth her lade,
>   Methinkes that gull did use his term as fit
>   Which termde his love a Giant for her wit.

Therefore, in his revision of 1599 Drayton arbitrarily changed the Nine Worthies from men to women, so that Idea's position in the sonnet would be more decorous.

In Sonnets 3 and 42, although a slight bitterness is displayed, he gave a moderate rebuff to his critics. However, when in Sonnets 31 and 46 his bitterness erupted, he violently castigated them as men who have failed to appreciate love. Both of these sonnets are very strong and effective, but 46 seems to offer the best choice of insults:

> Thou leaden Brain, which censur'st what I write,
> And say'st, my Lines be dull, and do not move;
> I marvel not, thou feel'st not my delight,
> Which never felt'st my fiery touch of Love;
> But thou, whose Pen hath like a Pack-Horse serv'd,
> Whose Stomack unto Gall hath turn'd thy Food,
> Whose Senses, like poor Pris'ners, hunger-starv'd,
> Whose Grief hath parch'd thy Body, dry'd thy Blood;
> Thou which hast scorned Life, and hated Death,
> And in a moment Mad, Sober, Glad, and Sorry;
> Thou which hast bann'd thy Thoughts, and curst thy Breath,
> With thousand Plagues, more then in Purgatory:
>   Thou, thus whose Spirit Love in his fire refines,
>   Come thou and read, admire, applaud my Lines.

This edition of 1599 resulted from the most meticulous and complete revision. From this point on Drayton did not change the basic sequence of the lyrics. Some sonnets were dropped; new ones took their place. Perhaps the remaining sonnets moved up or down a place or two in the numbering. All of Drayton's aims for this edition were to be continued in the subsequent revisions.

He had tried to reduce the excessive Petrarchisms which were then going out of fashion. This he accomplished by his omissions and new selections and revisions. He desired to write more vigorous sonnets, and this he did with the aid of his dramatic abilities. He sought to achieve variety, and he succeeded in this by adding new poems with differing topics, metaphors, and emotions. He aimed at regularization of his form, and he did this by cutting out the alexandrines, and holding the lines to pentameter with more popular rhyme schemes. He desired to write with greater coherence, and in this he was partially successful as he pruned many of the honey-sweet exclamations and apostrophes and rhetorical repetition in his attempt to achieve the direct speech of the drama. And by simplifying his diction and smoothing out his meter, he was enabling himself to overcome his worst habit, syntactical obscurity.

This revision of 1599 was the most significant and the most radical. In it were the seeds of the tones, attitudes, and techniques of the later edition, as he held on to the same basic aims in his future revisions. From this edition on, Drayton's sonnets are neither trials of skill nor exercises, but lyrics worthy of any of his contemporaries who wrote in this genre.

III Idea (*1600*), (*1602*)

In 1600 Drayton issued another revision of his sonnets under the short title of *Idea*, as he had changed it in 1599. The changes were by no means as great as they had been in 1599. Only one sonnet was excluded, "Sweete sleepe so arm'd with Beauty's arrows darting." Sonnet 20, "Stay, Stay sweet Time, behold or ere thou passe," which had line 14 rewritten in 1599, had four more lines rewritten for this edition. Many of the other revisions, minor though they were, were in keeping with Drayton's aim to improve the coherence of his lines by simplifying the syntax and diction and smoothing the meter.

In the previous revision he had titled several sonnets, and he continued this practice. Thus four of the older sonnets were given headings: 22, "To Humour"; 36, "To the River Ankor"; 52, "Another to the River Ankor"; and 9, "To Harmony." Two of the new sonnets also received tags: 12, "To Lunacy"; and 65, "To the Lady L. S."

The important change in this edition was the inclusion of eight new sonnets. With the exception of 62, in praise of the poet King James of Scotland, and 65, in praise of the Lady L. S., the new sonnets all seem to have an air of bitterness or critical cynicism.

In Sonnet 12, "As other Men, so I my self do Muse," he called himself "Lunatike" for having spent nine years writing love poetry "wresting invention so" and using "giddy metaphors." The sonnet has as its theme madness caused by poetic rather than erotic love. Pearson suggests that this sonnet, like 44, "Why do I speak of Joy, or write of Love," is perhaps a criticism of the excesses of the love-sick sonneteers, or perhaps an analysis of the disease of love itself.[22]

In Sonnet 27, "I hear some say, this Man is not in love," Drayton once again attacked the critics of his poetry who denied the truth of his love and the depth of his poetic passion. But the attack in this sonnet is mild in comparison with the violence he uttered in 1599 in "Thou leaden brain," and "Methinks I see some crooked Mimick jeer." In 31, "To such as say, Thy love I over-prize," he again restated his love for Idea in defiance of the critics.

In Sonnet 25 Drayton took a sly punch at the critics of his work. Seemingly he laughed at himself in classifying himself as a fool or child, yet the concluding couplet unsheathed the hidden barb:

> With Fools and Children good discretion bears;
> Then honest People, bear with Love and Me,
>
> .   .   .   .
>
> Love still a Baby, playes with Gawdes and Toys,
> And like a Wanton, sports with ev'ry Feather.
>
> .   .   .   .
>
> You that behold us, laugh us not to scorn,
> Give Nature thanks, you are not such as we:
> Yet Fools and Children sometime tell in play,
> Some wise in show, more Fools indeed then they.

In Sonnet 17, "If He, from Heav'n that filch'd that living fire," Drayton drew upon the myth of Prometheus stealing fire for the benefit of mankind. He gave an unusual twist to the analogy he

draws by making Idea the thief of his love, he then drew a
cynical observation about this kind of thievery:

> Which taking thence, you have escap'd away,
> Yet stand as free as ere you did before:
>> Yet old Prometheus punish'd for his Rape.
>> Thus poore Thieves suffer, when the greater scape.

A far departure from his highly embellished lyrics in 1594,
which were overladen with cloying sentiment, is Sonnet 57. Its
dramatic interchange of proverbs and aphorisms is closer to the
Native tradition than almost any other sonnet he had published
to date, and it graphically illustrates the distance he has moved
away from the completely Petrarchan sonnet:

> As Love and I, late harbour'd in one inn,
> With Proverbs thus each other entertain:
>> In Love there is no lack, thus I begin,
>> Fair words makes Fools, replyeth he again;
>> That spares to speak, doth spare to speed (quoth I)
>> As well (sayth he) too forward, as too slow;
>> Fortune assists the boldest, I reply,
>> A hasty Man (quoth he) ne'r wanted Woe;
>> Labour is light, where Love (quoth I) doth pay,
>> (Saith he) Light Burthen's heavy, if far borne;
>> (Quoth I) The Main lost, cast the By away;
>> You have spun a fair Thread, he replies in scorn.
> And having thus awhile each other thwarted,
> Fools as we met, so Fools again we parted.

In 1602 the only change was the insertion of one new sonnet,
41, thereby moving the last twenty-six sonnets of the 1600 edition one number farther on:

Sonnet 41 (1602)

> Dear, why should you command me to my Rest,
> When now the Night doth summon all to sleep?
> Me thinks this Time becometh Lovers best;
> Night was ordain'd, together Friends to keep:
> How happy are all other living Things,
> Which though the Day disjoin by sev'ral flight,
> The quiet Ev'ning yet together brings,

And each returns unto his Love at Night?
O, Thou that art so courteous unto all!
Why shouldn'st thou, Night, abuse me only thus,
That ev'ry Creature to his kind do'st call,
And yet 'tis thou do'st only sever us?
  Well could I wish, it would be ever Day,
  If when Night comes, you bid me go away.

The editions of 1600 and 1602 continued the process of growth
and change in Drayton's sonnets in the same direction as established in 1599. He more and more abandoned mere conven-
tionality and approached an interpretation of human reality.

IV Idea (1605)

When Drayton published the next revision of his sonnet sequence in 1605 he excluded four of the older sonnets. "These
tears quench hope, do kindle my desire," an original lyric completely rewritten for 1599, "My love makes hot the fire whose
heat is spent" from 1594, and "Eyes with your tears, blind if you
be" from 1599 were dropped because of the excessive emotion,
tears, and lamentation which they depicted. "My Fair, had I not
erst adorned the lute" from 1594 was excluded because of its
insistence on the divine powers of Idea. All of these lyrics were
well in keeping with the Petrarchan conventions which marked
his early sonnets; but as Drayton wrote on and began to compose
sonnets more marked for their realism and dramatic quality, these
early examples of Petrarchism became more and more out of
place in the sequence.

Seven new sonnets were inserted among the last twenty-one
of the sequence, and each of these was to be retained in his final
choice. Indeed, with the exception of the sonnet in praise of
King James all of the new sonnets from 1600 on survived the
weeding out process. The mood of these new sonnets is a quiet
one. Drayton did not seem to be concerned with the critics any
longer, and the bitterness of 1600 seems to have disappeared. He
now offered a peaceful sublimation of sentiment.

Thus in Sonnet 46, "Plain-path'd experience, th'unlearneds
guide," he utilized the common theme of his heart's murder at
the hands of his mistress. But he added a new note. The basic
metaphor is a medieval murder trial where the suspected mur-

derer is brought before the body of his victim. If the confronted person is the murderer, the corpse will start to bleed. And so it occurs in this sonnet. However, the poet seems to ask mercy on her behalf in the couplet: "But what of this? Should she to death be led,/If furthers Justice, but helpes not the dead." In Sonnet 50, "As in some Countries, far remote from this," his mistress torments him: "By curing me, and killing me each How'r,/Only to shew her Beauty's Sov'raigne Power," in the same way that surgeons use the living bodies of condemned felons to test their various poisons:

> First make incision on each mast'ring Vein,
> Then staunch the bleeding, then trans'pierce the Coarse,
> And with their Balms recure the Wounds again;
> Then Poison, and with Physic him restore.

Again in Sonnet 58 Drayton spoke of the subterranei, the spirits who guard buried treasure to prevent its discovery and removal. He saw this same hoarding of treasure in the way Idea guarded and hoarded her love:

> Ev'n as this Spirit, so you alone do play
> With those rich Beauties Heav'n gives you to keep;
> Pitty so left, to the coldness of your Blood,
> Not to avail you, nor do others good.

These last three sonnets illustrate a new trait which was appearing in his poetry; that is, he used abstruse facts upon which to build a metaphor. As these three sonnets have as their theme the cruelties and the coldness of his mistress, so in Sonnet 43 he complained of her abuse. He compared his condition to one who is in total darkness with no ray of light to greet him, and he used further an excellent image:

> So doth the Plow-man gaze the wand'ring Starre,
> And only rest contented with the Light
> That never learn'd what Constellations are,
> Beyond the bent of his unknowing Sight.
>
> .   .   .   .
>
> Would to God I were as ignorant as they. . . .

In Sonnet 47, "In pride of Wit, when high desire of Fame,/Gave Life and Courage to my lab'ring Pen," Drayton told of his success as a playwright, but disclaimed it since:

> No publik Glorie vainly I pursue,
> All that I seek, is to eternize you.

And in 57 he offered praise to her for her virtues and grace "Whose dear remembrance in my Bosom lies."

And finally in Sonnet 51, "Calling to mind since first my Love begun," Drayton used the events of the changing world of the last six years as an antithesis for the unchangeability of his love:

> Thus the World doth, and evermore shall Reel:
> Yet to my Goddesse am I constant ever;
> How e're blind Fortune turn her giddie Wheel:
> > Though Heaven and Earth, prove both to me untrue,
> > Yet am I still inviolate to You.

In this way the edition of 1605 with its seven new sonnets continued Drayton's move away from empty conventions toward dramatic illustrations of his motif of love.

V   Idea (1619)

In 1619 Drayton published his last revision of his sonnet sequence. In it is his final choice which he made from sonnets written over a period of more than twenty-five years. At this time he dropped fifteen of his sonnets which had appeared in earlier editions and transferred one, "The world's faire Rose, and Henries frosty fire," a catalog of the lovers in his epistles, to the conclusion of *England's Heroicall Epistles* where it belonged. In earlier editions it had served as a link between the epistles and *Idea*, which had been published together. Three of the excluded sonnets were addressed to individuals: "To King James"; "To Lucie, Countess of Bedford"; and "To Anne Harrington" (Lucie's mother). At this time Drayton was unhappy with the sad lot of poetry under the rule of King James. (Drayton satirized the King for this in *The Owle.*) Also he was no longer on the best of terms with the Bedford clan.

Of the other twelve which were excluded, most had counterparts and parallels in other contemporary sonnet sequences, and they had also been written when he was influenced by the works of Daniel, Sidney, and Barnes to write sonnets encrusted with heavy Petrarchan conceits, generally emphasizing his youthful sorrowing passion. Thus (using the numbering of 1605) 4, 6, 15, and 52 had similarities with *Delia* 29, 47, 4, and 21, and 27, 1, 8, 21, and 48 had parallels in *Parthenophil* 51, 77, 78, and 67.[23] He also excluded Sonnet 64 which had been the dedicatory sonnet in 1594, for he needed no longer to apologize for his "rude unpolish'd rymes" nor to protest his originality.

The ten new sonnets which were added in the final edition continued the attitudes of 1605. He repeated his motif of unchangeable love for Idea, but he did so in a mature, anti-sentimental manner. The major difference of the new sonnets from the ones dropped was that instead of using the general abstractions, conventional images, and a highly rhetorical diction constituting his Petrarchan habit in the 1590's, he used metaphors which drew real and vivid pictures with purposeful detail and forceful, relatively unadorned diction. He gave his metaphors a new dimension which had a depth reaching into real human existence. Thus in Sonnet 1, "Like an adventurous Seafarer am I," Drayton employed a simile used innumerable times, but here he added specific simple details which gave it strength and vigor:

> How far he sayl'd, what Countries he had seen,
> Preceding from the Port whence he put forth,
> Shows by his Compass, how his Course he steer'd,
> When East, when West, when South, and when by North,
> As how the Pole to ev'ry place was rear'd,
> What Capes he doubled, of what Continent,
> The Gulphs and Straits, that strangely he had past,
> Where most becalmed, where with foul Weather spent,
> And on what Rocks in peril to be cast?

And in Sonnet 6, "How many paltry, foolish, painted things," Drayton indicated the very real dislike and disgust he had for the dissolute women of James's court. In the first quatrain his anger came through, but it was quickly subdued as he turned his attention to Idea. And he offered some of his most nearly perfect lines, simple and direct, but containing deep poetic feeling:

> Where I to thee Eternity shall give,
> When nothing else remaineth of these days,
> And Queens hereafter shall be glad to live
> Upon the Alms of thy superfluous prayse;

. . . .

> So shalt thou fly above the vulgar Throng,
> Still to survive in my immortal Song.

In Sonnet 8 he revealed a very human attitude when, in taking the romantic theme of the ashes of beauty in old age, he did not follow the customary "carpe diem" which looked back with nostalgia to the days of fleeting youth, beauty, and love. Instead Drayton was almost savage in his depiction of Idea in decrepitude. The sonneteer seemed to glow with an ironical delight at the thought of time-ravaged Idea gazing into her mirror. The over-accent on detail almost shocks the reader. Somehow the element of playful humor usually found in this kind of reversal of the beauty lyric seems to be missing.

The same element of irony is present in Sonnet 15, "Since to obtain thee, nothing will me stead,/I have medicine that shall cure my Love." The medicine is a recipe for an awful potion made up of powder ground from her dead heart, her unfelt tears, and her dying sighs. This will produce a "remedy for Love." This medieval witches' brew almost moves the lyric into the realm of the macabre.

In Sonnet 21 Drayton turned the irony upon himself. He told how he wrote a sonnet on behalf of "A witless Gallant" to a young wench who was thus won. Yet all the poetry which Drayton had written on his own behalf had failed its purpose: "Yet by my Froth, this Fool his Love obtains,/And I lose you, for all my Wit and Pains." In two of the new sonnets he attacked Cupid for not assisting him in his quest for success in love. The last couplet of 36 showed an almost Cavalier attitude when he said: "I conjure thee by all that I have nam'd,/To make her love, or Cupid be thou damn'd." The same attitude is apparent in the opening line, and indeed, throughout Sonnet 48: "Cupid, I hate thee, which I'd have thee know." This is hardly the Petrarchan attitude which some critics claim to be Drayton's only poetic technique.

We have, in Sonnet 52, the Petrarchan conceit of the exchange of hearts which Drayton also used in his ode "The Heart." But the Petrarchism is in the conceit alone; the technique rises beyond mere convention when by simple and direct language Drayton managed to convey strength, self-possession, and seriousness beyond the surface pretense of anger:

> What do'st mean to Cheat me of my Heart
> To take all Mine, and give me none again?
> Or have thine Eyes such Magic, or that Art,
> That what They get, They ever do retain,
> Play not the tyrant, but take some Remorse,
> Rebate thy Spleen, if but for Pitty's sake.

Finally, the last new sonnet of the 1619 edition all critics justly consider to be Drayton's masterpiece in sonnetry:

> Since ther's no helpe, Come let us kiss and part,
> Nay, I have done: You get no more of Me,
> And I am glad, yea glad with all my heart,
> That thus so cleanly, I mySelf can free,
> Shake hands for ever, Cancel all our Vows,
> And when we meet at any time again,
> Be it not seen in either of our Brows,
> That we one jot of former Love retain;
> Now at the last gasp, of Loves latest Breath,
> When his Pulse failing, Passion speechless lies,
> When Faith is kneeling by his bed of Death,
> And Innocence is closing up his Eyes,
>   Now if thou would'st, when all have given him over,
>   From Death to Life, thou might'st him yet recover.

The octet contains a dramatic plea spoken in a simple and colloquial manner; then suddenly there is an unexpected picture drawn with the personified Love lying at the point of death and surrounded by the figures of Faith and Innocence. This allegorical tableau becomes a perfect transition for the final couplet and in effect binds the couplet more closely with the octet. George Saintsbury believed this sonnet to be one of the finest in existence, but he felt that it was beyond Drayton's capabilities and ought perhaps be attributed to Shakespeare.[24] Mario Praz agreed with Dante Gabriel Rossetti's insistence that it was the finest sonnet in the language.[25] I consider that this sonnet is actually a perfect culmination of long years of conscious effort in sonnet writing to develop lyrics of personal originality with definite dramatic qualities.

When we look carefully at the many sonnet sequences which were published by the English Renaissance poets, we can see that Drayton's large body of sonnets holds a unique place. Among all of the Elizabethans who wrote in this genre, his cover the longest period and show the growth and maturity occurring in a poet's style and techniques within a single genre. If the 1594 edition were all that we possessed, Drayton, as a sonneteer, would be thought a second-rate Petrarchist. If we had only the 1619 edition, he would be considered a highly effective dramatic lyricist. But since we have before us all of his editions, and since we can see how he pruned, trimmed, completely rewrote, excluded, and included new ideas and techniques over a quarter of a century, we can well maintain that he has made an invaluable contribution to the field of poetry.

Among the poets of his day he was held in high esteem for his poetic abilities. And today when we examine his sequence with its many changes and variants, we cannot fail to be impressed with his tremendous growth as a sonneteer. Although the early Drayton sonnets are highly imitative, some of the Petrarchan lyrics are gems of their kind; and each of his later editions became progressively more and more nearly excellent until the magnificent culmination of 1619.

CHAPTER 2

The Pastoral and Fairy Poetry

DRAYTON wrote much and well in another genre extremely popular with the late Elizabethans, the pastoral. Under the guise of writing about lowly shepherds and their love life, the Renaissance poets propounded their views on many subjects. They wrote about their own lives, made topical references, satirized the church or politics, told simple stories, and experimented with the language and various poetic techniques.

However, the pastoral was by no means an English-born genre. In an address to the reader, Drayton pointed out its Classical and European roots. He gave appropriate credit to Theocritus, Vergil, and Sannazaro as the chief pastoralists in the Greek, Roman, and European traditions. The pastoral was a highly popular genre on the continent during the late Middle Ages and the Renaissance. The works in this genre of Mantuan, Petrarch, Guarini, Tasso, and Marot, all carried over and influenced the English in their own development of the pastoral.

The first important pastoral in England in this period was Spenser's *The Shepherd's Calendar* in 1579.[1] In the 1590's Sir Philip Sidney and the Countess of Pembroke's (his sister) *Arcadia* as well as Thomas Lodge's *Rosalynde* made a strong and delightful impact on the English reader. Among the many pastorals arose romances, drama, satire, and elegy, all under the guise of the simple bucolic world.

In the same manner as he had done with the sonnet sequence, Drayton joined the ranks of the pastoralists in the early years of their popularity. In 1593 he published *Idea, The Shepheards Garland,* which was strongly influenced by Spenser's *Calendar.* Again just as he revised his sonnets until he arrived at new and original poems with greater maturity and polish, so he continued to work in the pastoral medium until he achieved like results. In 1595 he published *Endimion and Phoebe,* a pastoral with strong

Ovidian strains. He completely revised the 1593 edition of his eclogues in 1606 under the title of *Eclogs*, and at the same time rewrote the Endimion story under the heading of *The Man in the Moon*.

Long after the tide of popularity for the pastoral had receded Drayton again published several new works in this genre: *The Quest of Cynthia; The Shepheards Sirena*; and *Nimphidia*. Finally in 1630, the year before his death, he published his pastoral masterpiece, *The Muses Elizium*. In these works Drayton moved from the Elizabethan pastoral of Spenser and Lodge into a Caroline fairy pastoral which was completely original with him.

I Idea, The Shepheards Garland (*1593*)

In this his first pastoral work Drayton followed many of the same objectives which Spenser had had in the creation of *The Shepherd's Calendar*. Much of the style, the mood, the contrasting of types, and the love-sick debates are similar in both works. Thus Rowland bewails his unrequited love as did Colin. Drayton's eclogues I and IX have the same basic subject as January and December in that both are complaints. Eclogue II and February come together in a debate between old age and youth. In Eclogue III there is a panegyric to Queen Elizabeth as in April; also the elegy for Sir Philip Sidney in Eclogue V has certain similarities with the elegy for Dido in October. The subjects and the sentiments are frequently the same in both works, and Drayton used many of the metrical patterns which occurred in Spenser's pastoral. Spenser had used archaisms to discover a language suitable for poetry; Drayton used many of the same archaisms, but added more of them from the Midland dialect.

However, Drayton did not merely copy Spenser. The two works have completely different purposes. Spenser had used the pastoral tradition, as handed down from Petrarch and Mantuan, to attack religious and political abuses. Drayton had no specific target for attack; he observed society and made general comments on it at times. In addition Drayton emphasized the English background of his characters by drawing a fictional world which could easily fit into the Cotswolds. Furthermore, Spenser developed his *Calendar* around the changing of the seasons and Colin's change from youth to age, while Drayton did not follow the seasons with any consistency. Actually the arrangement of the *Garland* was in a rough concentric pattern. Eclogues I and IX were monologues of complaint; II and VII were debates on love between youth and age; and the center formed a core of four eclogues with panegyrics. Drayton, unlike Spenser, turned away from archaic dialect for the most part, and emphasized it only in the ballad in VIII.

In Eclogue I the shepherd "Rowland malcontent bewayles/ the winter of his grief" (ll. 3-4). But the tone of the poem is not merely that of unrequited love as in January. Rowland's complaint is coupled with deep religious significance and imagery. He calls on "O Blessed Pan," here the Christian God, for merciful attention to his confession. The first half of the eclogue contains the ritualistic pattern of submission, contrition, and oblation:

> Let smoky sighs be pledges of contribution
> For Follies past to make my souls submission.
>
> ll. 47-48

The eclogue opens in spring, and the freshness of the season provides a contrast for his melancholy and repentance. In the *Calendar* Colin moved from disappointment mingled with hope in "January" to complete despair in "December"; but Rowland does not show this progression. Rather he begins in I with pious repentance and ends in IX with hopeless lovesickness. The IXth eclogue takes place in winter, and the weather corresponds to Rowland's somber state. In this eclogue he calls on Phoebe and the stars to hear his complaint. In both I and IX Drayton used the sixain, *ababcc*, the metrical form of Spenser's January and December.

Eclogues II and VII are debates on the pros and cons of love as exemplified by the attitudes of brash youth and calm old age. In II Winken and Motto refer to the fable of the oak and the briar from Spenser's "February"; but, whereas in Spenser the oak is mighty and strong, in Drayton it is a symbol of death and decay. Here there is no quarrel between the two, only a contrast between beauty and decay, between youthful heedlessness and bitter experience. Winken, who is perhaps Wynken de Word representing the wisdom of literature, rebukes the idolatrous attitude of love-sick Rowland, who has praised his human mistress in terms befitting only God's infinite virtues. On the other hand, the youthful Motto praises the divine inspiration of poetry and love which lifts man to the highest heavens. Basically the lines of the debate are drawn between Winken's moralistic view of love as a worldly vanity, and Motto's Platonic ideal of love.

Again in the VIIth eclogue a debate takes place as

> Borrill an aged shepheard swaine,
>   with reasons doth reproove,
> Batte a foolish wanton boy,
>   but lately fall'n in love.

ll. 1-4

The elder shepherd also defends the quiet life of the retired against the youth's plea for the Platonic ideal of love. The debate can also be interpreted as one between the contemplative life of literature and the active life of the senses. One of the delightful sections of the eclogue is Borrill's listing of the curses which love can bring to its votaries:

> Oh spightfull wayward wretched love,
> Woe to Venus which did nurse thee,
> Heavens and earth thy plagues do prove,
> Gods and men have cause to curse thee.
> Thoughts grief, hearts woe,
> Hopes pain, bodies languish,
> Envies rage, sleeps foe,
> Fancies fraud, souls anguish,
> Desires dread, minds madness,
> Secrets betrayer, natures error,
> Sights deceit, sullens sadness,
> Speeches expense, Cupids terror,
> Malcontents melancholly,
> Lives slaughter, deaths nurse,
> Cares slave, dotards folly,
> Fortunes bait, worlds curse,
> Looks theft, eyes blindness,
> Selfs will, tongues treason,
> Pains pleasure, wrongs kindness,
> Furies frensy, follies reason:

> With cursing thee as I began,
> Cursing thee I make an end,
> Neither God, neither man,
> Neither Fairy, neither Fiend.
>
> ll. 127-50

Then Batte gives a listing of all the virtues which the power of Platonic love can bring as an answer to this curse. It is interesting to note that all of the women to whom Batte refers in his list come from Chaucer's *Legend of Good Women.*

In Eclogue III Rowland and Perkin discuss the fair Beta, Queen Elizabeth, and Rowland sings a panegyric in her honor. In the dialogue preceding the song, Drayton used an unusual metrical scheme in which he connects the rhyme in pairs of quatrains, *abbc cdda,* and the fourth lines of each quatrain are in dimeter rather than the pentameter which precedes. In his introduction Rowland professes to scorn flattery, and humbly promises to speak only the truth in his panegyric. In this song Drayton used all of the paraphernalia which was in Spenser's April. The river Thames is presented as the unifying factor of the song and of England. The maiden queen is connected with the stream of English history as she is hailed, "Alone the Phenix is, of all thy watery brood." Rowland proclaims her political prowess as the personification of England, and the entire fairy populace of the river sing out in an orchestration in Beta's praise. Finally Rowland deifies Beta as he makes a patriotic challenge to all of England's foes.

In Eclogue IV Winken bewails the loss of Elphin, Sir Philip Sidney, in two songs. Before the dirges begin, Gorbo refers to the great literature of England as represented by Wynken de Word and Chaucer:

> Come sit we down . . .
> And tell a tale of Gawen or Sir Guy,
>   Of Robin Hood, or of good Clem a Clough.
>
> Or else some Romant unto us agreed,
>   Which goode olde Godfrey taught thee in thy youth,
> Of noble Lords and Ladies gentle deed,
>   Or of thy love, or of thy lasses truth.
>
> ll. 33-40

Winken then begins his dirge for Elphin. The best lines in the eclogue are the description of Elphin:

> A heavenly clowded in a human shape,
>> Rare substance, in so rough a bark Iclad,
> Of Pastorall, the lively spring in sappe,
>> Thou mortall thou, thy fame immortall made.

ll. 58-61

Then Winken sings Rowland's elegy for Elphin. This is in the traditional manner as he recalls Elphin's birth, accomplishments, death, and final rebirth as a shepherd.

In Eclogue V Motto compares the false nobility of inherited prestige and wealth with the true nobility of "Fortunes Orphanes," poets, who have the prestige and wealth of talent. He boasts of the poet's spiritual ancestors and his heritage of divine inspiration. Rowland then descries the evils of dissimulation and flattery which exist in the court, and prepares to sing faithfully of the glories of Idea, who together with Beta and Pandora is exempt from pride of birth and flattery. In a horribly strained series of conceits Rowland describes the beauty of Idea.

In Eclogue VI Perkin and Gorbe contrast the aristocrats of yesteryear who practiced virtue with the contemporaries who ignore it. These lines are reminiscent of those which Cuddie speaks in October. Then Perkin utters a long panegyric on Pandora, the Countess of Pembroke. This consists of a long group of extravagant conceits in which Drayton, usually a careful scholar and craftsman, confuses his mythology. Apollo-Phoebus becomes at once her father and her brother; and, in his praise, he seems to have forgotten that Pandora was mythologically the source of all the world's troubles.

In Eclogue VIII Drayton reached his zenith for the entire work. First Motto and Gorbo discuss contemporary poetry and the low conditions of those who sold their talents to the highest bidder, then he speaks of the glories of the Golden Age. Finally Motto sings the ballad of Dowsabell. In this ballad we hear the first strains of Drayton's exquisite fairy poetry. For his meter and rhyme he drew on Chaucer's *Sir Thopaz* and Spenser's *March* for a lilting rollicking effect. In this humorous rendition of the young English lady who wooed a shepherd, the jingling rhythm of the old romances does not seem forced or archaic, but rather it fits perfectly. Drayton here shows more humor than could be found in all of Spenser. And his characters, though placed in Arden, are thoroughly English:

> Her feature all as fresh above,
> As is the grass that growes by Dove,
>   as lyth as lass of Kent:
> Her skin as soft as Lemster wooll,
> As white as snow on peakish hull,
>   or Swanne that swims in Trent.
>
> ll. 147-52

And the shepherd whom she sought was another from English soil:

> This shepheard ware a sheepe gray cloke,
> Which was of the finest loke,
>   that could be cut with sheere,
> His mittens were of Bauzens skin,
> His cockers were of Cordiwin,
>   his hood of Meniveere.
> His aule and lingell in a thong,
> His tar-boxe on his broad belt hong,
>   his breech of Colntrie blew:
> Full crispe and curled were his lockes,
> His brows as white as Albion rocks,
>   so like a lover true.
>
> ll. 177-88

In "Dowsabell" Drayton never gave the reader quite what might be expected. He discovered and exploited the comic principle of emphasized incongruity. It is this very unpredictability which makes the ballad so pleasing to read. The blend of the aristocratic and the humble, the frequent and unexpected change of the pursuer into the pursued, and the archaic language with the metrical form of *Sir Thopaz* make up a lyric which anyone could enjoy. And the last part has a delight all its own as Dowsabell succumbs to the one she had sought to seduce:

> With that she bent her snow-white knee,
> Downe by the shepheard kneeled she,
>   and him she sweetly kist.
> With that the shepheard whoop'd for joy,
> Quoth he, ther's never shepheards boy,
>   that ever was so blist.
>
> ll. 237-42

[51]

In general Drayton followed the leadership of Spenser in his first pastoral, but he also made several of his own contributions to the growth of the form. He dropped the extremes of political or religious satire, and made the pastoral primarily a series of discussion and songs in praise of love, friendship, and the Golden Age. He also restored a sense of humor to the pastoral which recalled some of the Theocritan comic idylls.

Specifically his first attempt at this genre had its drawbacks. The eclogues were filled with many awkward constructions and violent inversions of syntax. In order to maintain the meter and rhyme, he frequently had subjects without verbs and used participles as main verbs. Also many of the conceits were overly extravagant and strained. It would be his task in his coming revisions to eliminate these faults which were common to most of his early poetry. Of the entire series, "Dowsabell" alone needed and received little revising.

II Eclogs (*1606*)

Thirteen years after their first publication, a completely revised edition of the pastoral *Garland* appeared under the simple title of *Eclogs*. Drayton rewrote almost all of the songs, transposed the sequence, and added another eclogue to the set. Other changes included the dropping of the verse arguments which had prefaced each eclogue and the Latin tags from Ovid's *Amores* which had followed each eclogue. He also changed his rule against allowing the same character to appear in successive eclogues.[2]

A few changes were made in this edition for the republication in 1619, but these were mostly for the purpose of improving the versification and the syntax. In each of the newer versions Drayton smoothed out the lines by cutting down on the complexity of the rhetoric. His efforts were not completely successful, but the trend of his revisions is easily observed. Drayton did strain the rhythm in a few places (i.e., Borrill's curse on love in 7:131-46), but this was the exception rather than the rule. An analysis of the 1619 variants shows that Drayton changed relatively few rhymes. Actually the basic revisions which Drayton made were paralleling the new Jacobean fashion in writing which was moving away from the extravagant and self-conscious mannerisms of the Elizabethans. He reworked most of the heavy conceits to bring the rhetoric into better balance with the ideas which were the rational element of the poems. He also dropped many of the archaisms with the exception of Eclogue VII, making a greater contrast and effectiveness in their use in the "Dowsabell" segment. In this edition Drayton was not really departing from the Spenserian influence; rather, he was following the master of *Colin Clouts Come Home Again.* For Spenser had, in this later work, led the pastoralists away from their fascination with rhetoric and bombast which had occupied their interests in the early 1590's.

In Eclogue I Drayton dropped his use of the repentance theme which had held such a dominant place in Eclogue I of the earlier edition. Instead of this religious emphasis, Rowland emphasizes his defiance as a poet who has failed to receive adequate recognition. Of course we are well aware of Drayton's bitter disappointment in not being recognized in some signal way at the accession of King James to the throne in 1603.

In the last eclogue Drayton made extensive internal changes with only seven of the seventeen stanzas recognizable from 1593. No longer is the emphasis on Rowland as the forlorn lover, but rather Rowland points to the stars as the cause of his difficulties. He also carries on the theme of Eclogue I as a poet of injured merit and frustrated ambition. He achieved an excellent mood of tranquillity in two of the stanzas in which he emphasizes his own poetic abilities:

> O Night, how still obsequious have I been
> To thy slow silence whispering in thine ear,
> That thy pale Sovereign often hath been seen,
> Stay to behold me sadly from her Sphere,
>   Whilst the slow minutes duly I have told,
>   With watchfull eyes attending on my Fold.
> How oft by thee the solitary Swain,
> Breathing his passion to the early spring,
> Hath left to hear the Nightingale complain,
> Pleasing his thoughts alone, to hear me sing!
>   The Nymphs forsook their places of abode,
>   To hear the sounds that from my Music flow'd.

> ll. 31-42

In Eclogue II Drayton no longer attributed the virtues of the divinity to Idea, but he does make her the *primum mobile* of the universe; and the general emphasis shifts to the worship of women. The second song becomes a deification of love itself. In this latter song he introduced a new form of eight-line stanza with the first four lines, a pentameter quatrain, *abab*, and the second four, a ballad quatrain, tetrameter-trimeter, *cdcd*.

In his praise of Beta in Eclogue IV Drayton made a few very significant changes which strengthened the structure of the poem. He made the Thames a King, better to balance Beta, Queen of the Virgins. He deleted the stanzas on the Muses and the angels, so that all of the emphasis would fall on the homage of the nymphs. He also added certain dramatic qualities of action to the poem. The nymphs now enter singing and announce Beta's arrival; they sport on the strand while Beta reclines on the bank. Beta peers into the water and sees her own reflection, and thus the sea deities have better reason to spread her fame as it has been caught by the waters. These bits of action make the poem more realistic, and take away much of the artificiality caused by the conventions in such a panegyric.

In V he revised his panegyric to Idea, giving a new order to the jumble of praises of her features. Now the poem has a real sense of direction as he carefully praises her physical self in five stanzas leading to the stanzas which describe her real beauty, her virtues. Thus in an ascending order he moves from beauty to goodness.

Drayton converted the first dirge for Elphin in Eclogue VI from the struggle of man and death into a commentary on the present sorry state of poetry with a plea for the return to Sidney's poetic ideals. He presents King James as representative of degeneracy, false taste, courtly sycophancy, and obloquy opposed by Sidney as representative of the ancient virtues, true taste, honest courtly behavior, and final fame. He also praises Melibaeus (Samuel Daniel) and Alexis (Sir William Alexander) as true followers of the Sidney ideal.[3]

In Eclogue VIII he dropped the panegyric to Pandora and substituted a discussion of the virtues and the vices of nobility. In his revision Drayton made a clearer differentiation between the characters of Gorbo and Perkin than he had in 1593. Perkin now is clearly a stoic moralist, and Gorbo is a pupil who needs his doubts resolved. It now becomes a debate between two articulate points of view. Drayton also borrowed from *Colin Clouts Come Home Again* the idea of a list of ladies from the court, but he adds the original touch of identifying them by means of a river.

The entire chorus of shepherds celebrates a holiday in Eclogue IX. The mood of the piece is one of reality with concrete details giving a picture of the homely rural life. In it Drayton kept the language simple and unadorned and avoided an excess of mythological references. The shepherds are real and practical people, interested in the same things as the shepherds of the Cotwolds. The songs are light and playful with that deftness of touch which was to characterize Drayton's later pastoral works. The first "The Shepheards Daffadil" and the second, a duet between Motto and Perkin, had been included in *England's Helicon* in 1600 with several other of his pastoral lyrics. The third song deifies Idea and is sung by Rowland and the complete chorus. This panegyric has all of the qualities which are lacking in that of Eclogue V. It has real pastoral decorum with a definite sense of direction and plan as the poet moves from the praise of the physical to the final stanza in which she becomes "the shepheards starr."

III   Endimion and Phoebe

Three years after the original publication of *The Shepheards Garland* Drayton included another current trend in his pastoral poetry, that of the Ovidian or amatory. Among the many Ovidian poems which were published about this time were Christopher Marlowe's *Hero and Leander*—being circulated in manuscript by 1593—Shakespeare's *Venus and Adonis* and *The Rape of Lucrece*, and finally Drayton's *Endimion and Phoebe*.

In this work Drayton followed the lead of Shakespeare and Marlowe in the development of the Ovidian myth and combined with it DuBartas' expression of Platonic love as found in *Uranie*. The Drayton poem falls naturally into two parts. The first is a pastoral love story in which the goddess Phoebe disguises herself as a shepherdess and pursues Endimion until he in turn tries to catch her. Then she reveals her divinity, and the second part begins. Endimion is translated to Mount Latmus, the home of the Muses; and the poet gives a poetized scientific discourse on celestial numbers, astrology, and poetic inspiration. Endimion is taught to love natural beauty; but upon discovering Phoebe is absolute beauty, he is taken to heaven in order to visualize the Platonic ideal.

The first part of the poem is heavy with the Ovidian richness without being erotic. In Drayton's description of the shepherd and the moon goddess, many passages are immediately apparent as paralleling segments of Marlowe's *Hero and Leander*. The following verses, for instance, are closely modeled on Marlowe's description of Hero, although they are Drayton's description of Phoebe:

> An Azur'd Mantle purfled with a veil,
> Which in the Air puft like a swelling sail,
> Embosted Rainbows did appeare in silk,
> With way streams as white as mornings Milk:
> Which ever as the gentle Ayr did blow,
> Still with the motion seem'd to ebb and flow:
> About her neck a chain twice twenty fold,
> Of Rubies, set in lozenges of gold;
> Trust up in trammels, and in curious pleats,
> With spheary circles falling on her teats.
> A dainty smock of Cypress, fine and thin,
> Or'e cast with curls next to her Lilly skin:
>
> ll. 111-22

This appearance of Phoebe in her azure mantle is similar to DuBartas' *Uranie*, who appeared so clad, and who also suggested a journey about the stars in which the poet might learn the secrets of planetary lore and absorb the fire of poesy. Again the description of the clothes also reminds one of Belphoebe in Spenser's *Faerie Queene* (II, iii, 26).

Another Marlowian chord is struck when Jove is seized with passion for Endimion. In the second sestiad of *Hero and Leander*, although Neptune is well aware that Leander is a boy, the god is still stirred with passion for him. Also Endimion is here endowed with Hero's nectarous breath. The role of pursuer is not completely unlike the role of Venus in Shakespeare's poem. However she is not so persistent, and the erotic emphasis is greatly subdued. Finally she and Endimion reverse their roles of pursuer and pursued. These similarities do not mean that Drayton was merely borrowing from his contemporaries. In this new genre he had his own original contribution to make. He was able to take the richness and lushness of the Ovidian school and adapt it so that although the erotic element was diminished, its magnificence was not dimmed. Phoebe tempted Endimion, yet like Belphoebe who tempted Bragadoccio, she remained the very personification of chastity. Here the poet is being tested, and when he appreciates her beauty, she leads him to the perfection of the Platonic ideal.

The first part of the poem is excellent. Drayton managed to draw real and vivid pictures of the man and maid. His couplets, which are smoother than Marlowe's and which have, incidentally, a much higher rate of final closure, make the poem move swiftly along.

The last section of the poem is almost poetized science as Drayton turned from the Ovidian myth to an apology for poetry as the divine science. The joining of the two sections is not well done, and perhaps the poem would be a better pastoral if the second part had been omitted. After revealing her real identity and taking Endimion on his journey, Phoebe shows him the movement of the spheres and explains the effects of the conjunctions upon the fates of man. Then she takes him to the court of the Muses. Here he is crowned with bays, and a triumphal procession is arranged. The divine origin of poetry is affirmed; then Endimion is returned to earth with the promise of future visits from Phoebe.

The poem ends with praise to Spenser, Daniel, and Lodge as

> . . . the heyres of ever-living fame,
> The worthy titles of a Poets name,
> Whose skill and rarest excellence is such,
> As spitefull Envy never yet durst tuch.
>
> ll. 105-8

Then the poet pays his customary tribute to the "Sweet Nymph of *Ankor*." Although Drayton failed to mention Marlowe here, he later paid him the highest praise possible in his epistle to Henry Reynolds:

> Neat Marlow bathed in the Thespian Springs
> Had in him those brave translunary things,
> That the first Poets had, his raptures were,
> All air, and fire, which made his verses clear,
> For that fine madnes still he did retain,
> Which rightly should possesse a Poets brain.
>
> ll. 105-10

IV   The Man in the Moon

Endimion and Phoebe was never reprinted during Drayton's lifetime. Instead he rewrote the poem completely in 1606 with a new title, *The Man in the Moon*, and cut the old version almost in half. The love story of the first part was dropped; instead the poem opens with a pastoral scene in which the shepherds are celebrating the feast of Pan. At their request Rowland tells a story relating how Phoebe disguised herself to protect Endimion from the radiance of her divinity. He gives a long description of the mantle she wears. On it is depicted the violence of the sea, and waterfowl and their habitations. This painting on the mantle recalls the medieval tradition which Chaucer used when he described the paintings lining the walls of the temple of Mars in *The Knight's Tale*. The listing of the water-birds comes from Sylvester's translation of *La Semaine*; however, Drayton amplifies the catalog and gives such a realistic description of their habits as one might expect today from a member of the Audubon Society.

Phoebe comforts Endimion who is frightened by the pictures of violence on her mantle. She tells him of her ancestry and her powers as a goddess in ruling the tides of the sea, the fertility of the earth, and the minds of men. She then takes him on a much more orderly journey than in 1595. First they visit the haunts of the nymphs of the waters, the seas, the mountains, and the woods. From there they go on to the celestial spheres and the abode of the fixed stars and the angels. Finally, from the moon the poet looks down upon the earth where he sees the hidden vices of the miser, the lecher, the murderer, the thief, and the false lover.

The changes in the poem are numerous. Now the journey is taken only to instruct Endimion in the mysteries of the human condition and the universe. The melancholy which afflicts Endimion no longer proceeds from love, but from an inability to understand Phoebe and what she means. For in this new version he sees three contrasting worlds: the pleasant pastoral life of Rowland and the shepherds; the vicious underworld of the werewolves in the opening, and of evil men at the end; and the world of the nymphs and the celestial mysteries. The poet stands with the shepherds between the vicious and the celestial, and he has

the duty to report the beauties of the latter and expose the evils
of the former.

In 1595 the poem had the flavor of Spenser and Marlowe, but
now it has changed to a Jacobean simplicity in its description
and action. The extravagance of the Ovidian influence is gone,
but the poem does not suffer from this absence. Actually the new
structural unity and definite sense of direction which hold this
poem together far outbalance the loss of the love story. It is not
inferior to *Endimion and Phoebe*; it is rather another kind of
poetic rendition.

V   The Quest of Cynthia

In 1627 Drayton once again published a pastoral which might
be considered a third version of the Endimion story. In this short
poem of 232 lines written in the regular ballad form, an unnamed
shepherd is seeking a nymph called Cynthia, which is frequently
another name for the moon goddess. The setting is completely
pastoral and peaceful. The description of Cynthia's bower is a
distillation of the ideal pastoral landscape, and it offers its peace
and repose in opposition to the violence and evil rampant in the
real world. But this time the poet feels no need to correct or re-
prove the vices of mankind; he seeks only a haven of rest. The
love he feels for Cynthia is chaste, for she is the idealized mistress of the sonnet and the pastoral:

> Which spoke I felt such holy fires
>   To overspread my breast,
> As lent life to my Chaste desires
>   And gave me endless rest.
>   ll. 225-28

One of the best passages in this light poem is the description
of some of the creatures which inhabit the bower:

> The waxen Pallace of the Bee,
>   We seeking will surprise
> The curious workmanship to see,
>   Of her full laden thighs. . . .
>
> The nimble Squirrel noting here,
>   Her mossy dray that makes,
> And laugh to see the lusty Deer
>   Come bounding ore the brakes.

The Spiders web to watch we'll stand,
    And when it takes the Bee,
We'll help out of the tyrants hand,
    The Innocent to free.

Sometime we'll angle at the Brook
    The freckles Trout to take,
With silken Worms, and bait the hook,
    Which him our prey shall make.
                    ll. 188-92, 201-12

Like *Endimion and Phoebe* and *The Man in the Moon*, this playful pastoral is still a basic allegory of the poet's search for comfort and inspiration away from the known material world. In this work his Caroline style is as light and delicate as any of Herrick's.

<h2 style="text-align:center">VI The Shepheards Sirena</h2>

Another pastoral in the 1627 edition was *The Shepheards Sirena*. The story within the Sirena poem is almost nonexistent. The shepherd Dorilus reads a letter from his love Sirena which tells of her love for him and of the dangers she must face. Naturally this grieves Dorilus, and the shepherds cheer him with their song of the Trent. Finally, they warn him that the swineherds are about to attack the flocks and that he must cast off his poor spirits and join in the common defense. This seems to be a pastoral poem about the Golden Age. The lilting lines have a base of winter and heartbreak. The whole object of the poem seems to be a description of love and sorrow, with the object a woman, a river, or neither. It is Drayton's closest approach to the pure poetry of emotion without a definite object.

This 383 line poem has an unusual metrical form. The basic meter which is used throughout, except for the 170 lines of the song, consists of tetrameter heptasyllabic quatrains with an *abab* rhyme scheme. The song has ten stanzas of twelve lines with a common five line refrain:

On thy Bank,
In a Rank,
Let thy Swans sing her
And with their Music,
    along let them bring her.
                    ll. 177-81

Since it is a song, the lines could be considered to be a variable of the normal eleven syllable couplet with a masculine internal rhyme after the third beat. With this in mind, the chorus becomes another long couplet. However, considering the lightness of the poem and the fact that the regular line only has seven syllables, the song gives a better visual impression and the rhymes are emphasized with these short line divisions.

The poem as a whole is a delightful piece of writing. Its major quality is the smoothness of the line which almost hypnotizes the reader into belief in the sorrow and passion described. It also seems to have affinities with such works as Brown's *Shepherd's Pipe* and Wither's *Shepherd's Hunting*, which have the same delicate pastoral atmosphere but a stronger satiric flavor.

VII   Nimphidia, The Court of Fayrie

The best poem in the 1627 edition was his fairy poem, *Nimphidia*. Written in eighty-eight rollicking eight-line stanzas, it has an *aaabcccb* rhyme scheme. The *a* and *c* lines are generally regular tetrameter and the *b* lines are trimeter with a feminine ending. This shortened line with the feminine rhyme causes the tempo of the poem to move at a fast pace. In this mock heroic tale we have a burlesquing of many of the features of the medieval romance besides this variation of the meter. As a fairy tale *Nimphidia* does not really belong in the pastoral genre. However, in a study of Drayton's works it does represent one stage in his own development of the pastoral. This genre was basically escapist in nature. Love and romance in a humble rustic setting was the tone set for the pastoral by Theocritus. In this poem Drayton investigated an area of the woodland landscape familiar to all Englishmen from their folklore. He wrote of the love and romance of the fairies who were the "natural" inhabitants of the English countryside. Drayton merely emphasized this one aspect of the pastoral world in this poem.

Further *Nimphidia* represents a stage in his move to a more Classical pastoral world which he would later describe in *The Muses Elizium*. In this latter poem Drayton reached his ultimate in the pastoral genre. He retained the fairyland of *Nimphidia* and peopled it with nymphs and swains. Elizium finally moves beyond the land of magic into a land of the ideal. With the exception of the eighth nimphall which does emphasize the diminutiveness of the fairies, Drayton's nymphs and swains think and act like shepherdesses and shepherds of the Theocritan idylls. By passing through the fairyland of Queen Mab, Drayton was able to discover the ideal homeland, Elizium, for a pastoral setting.

Nimphidia is the story of love and madness at the court of Queen Mab. King Oberon discovers that Mab is entertaining the attentions of a would-be lover, Pigwiggen, and out of jealousy goes mad. In his frenzy he seeks out his humbler but more successful rival. Like Orlando Furioso he strikes out at everything he meets. However, in the diminutive world in which he lives all of his efforts have a hilarious result. He scourges a glow worm for carrying a fire in its tail; he charges into a beehive and is smeared with wax and honey; he is tossed from his war horse, an ant, into the dirt; he charges up a molehill and falls down the other side into a lake, a puddle, and the fall somewhat cools his temper. Next he charges Puck, or Hob the goblin, to seize the Queen. She repulses him with her magic incantations. Then Tomalin, as the King's champion, jousts with Pigwiggen. Finally Proserpina brings each of the chief figures a drink from the waters of Lethe. When they each take a sip, they forget the cause of their quarrels, and peace and harmony are once again restored to Queen Mab's court.

The poem includes all of the chivalric trappings of the more ancient romance with its knights in armor and the fair ladies of the court. The adventures of the fairy knights and the jousting are modeled on the deeds of those human knights of yore, but Drayton always causes the results of the quests and adventures to be laughable.

One of the most delightful sections concerns the arming of Pigwiggen in preparation for his joust with Tomalin:

> And quickly arms him for the Field,
> A little Cockle-shell his Shield,
> Which he could very bravely wield:
>   Yet could it not be pierced:
> His Spear a Bent both stiff and strong,
> And well-near of two Inches long;
> The Pyle was of a Horse-fly's tongue,
>   Whose sharpness naught reversed.

And puts him on a coat of Male,
Which was of a Fishes scale,
That when his Foe should him assail,
    No poynt should be prevayling:
His Rapier was a Hornets sting,
It was a very dangerous thing:
For if he chanc'd to hurt the King,
    It would be long in healing.

His Helmet was a Beetles head,
Most horrible and full of dread,
That able was to strike one dead,
    Yet did it well become him:
And for a plume, a horses hair,
Which being tossed with the air,
Had force to strike his Foe with fear,
    And turn his weapon from him.

Himself he on an Earwig set,
Yet scarce he on his back could get,
So oft and high he did corvet,
    Ere he himself could settle:
He made him turn, and stop, and bound,
To gallop, and to trot the Round,
He scarce could stand on any ground,
    He was so full of mettle.

ll. 489-520

Another passage which is almost irresistible is that in which Queen Mab casts a conjuration against Hob the goblin in lines 409-32. Unfortunately this piece did not lead to any great surge in the writing of fairy poems. Herrick was about the only important poet to carry on from Drayton in this genre. In *Oberon's Palace* in 1635 and *Hesperides* of 1648, he had a number of poems which were greatly influenced by Drayton's *Nimphidia*. However, the onslaught of the Puritan surge cut short these fanciful tales; for the Puritans considered such fairy work as tools of the devil and an invention of the papists.[4]

Drayton has much of the world of Shakespeare's *Midsummer Night's Dream* in this work, but he adds the burlesque and emphasizes the diminutive. He has the delicate control of Herrick's fairy poetry, only on a greater scale. Drayton's fairy world is not idealized, but rather everything is described in delightful specific detail with the fairies possessing very human passions and emotions. Aside from Herrick, the best passage in literature which illustrates the same quality as found in Drayton's poem is Mercutio's speech about Queen Mab in Act one, scene four, of *Romeo and Juliet*.

VIII The Muses Elizium

The year before he died Drayton published his last pastoral, *The Muses Elizium*, which consisted of a verse argument describing Elizium and ten nimphalls. It is a combination of true pastoral elegance with fairy lightness. The majority of the characters in Elizium are not shepherds, but rather nymphs; yet in this new work he moved closer to the Classical form of the pastoral than in any of his previous writings. In itself *The Muses Elizium* was Drayton's masterpiece in the delicate Caroline manner. He had by this time solved most of the problems which he had observed in his craftsmanship over the previous thirty-nine years. His style had finally become smooth, and the language now flowed with less effort than before. In it he handled many different metrical forms with true ease and grace. Thus scattered throughout the work are ballad quatrains, *abab*; tetrameter couplets; pentameter couplets; hexameter couplets; pentameter quatrains, *abab*; a double three-line stanza, *aabccb*, with tetrameter in *a* and *c* lines and trimeter in *b* lines; double trimeter quatrains linked together by the rhyme *aaab cccb*. In all of these there is new ease in their use.

In his description of Elizium Drayton drew a picture of a paganized New Jerusalem, a place of sanctity, reverence, and delight—indeed, a place of enchantment as in *The Tempest*. It is another Bower of Bliss, but one of abundance without the excess and condemnation of Spenser's:

> Where, in Delights that never face,
> The Muses lulled be,
> And sit at pleasure in the shade,
> Of many a stately tree,
>
> Which no rough tempest makes to reel
> Nor their straight bodies bows,
> Their lofty tops do never feel
> The weight of winters snows;
>
> ll. 5-12

The very flowers contend with one another in trying to excel in the perfume they exude as they blossom at any time. The season is always the best.

Elizium is also the special home of the poet, remote from the ordinary and close to the divine:

> The thrice three Virgins heavenly Clear,
> Their trembling Timbrels sound,
> Whilst the three comely Graces there
> Dance many a dainty Round,
>
> Decay nor Age there nothing knows
> There is continuall Youth,
> As Time on plant or creature grows,
> So still their strength renewth.
>
> The Poets Paradise this is,
> To which but few can come;
> The Muses only bower of bliss
> Their dear Elizium.
>
> Here happy souls, (their blessed bowers,
> Free from the rude resort
> Of beastly people) spend the hours,
> In harmeless mirth and sport,
>
> Then on to the Elizium plains
> Apollo doth invite you
> Where he provides with pastorall strains,
> In Nimphals to delight you.
>
> ll. 93-112

In the argument he concretized the pastoral landscape and prepared the reader for the games of emulation which are a keynote of the action in Elizium.

In the first nimphall the two nymphs Rodope and Dorida engage in a Theocritan singing match, but in this case the ladies are busy praising each other's beauty. They mingle in their compliments the things they really observe with some fulsome exaggerations. The mood of the piece is playful and hyperbolic (a common touch in Elizium) until the end when a note of human acidity appears as they are accused of dissimulation, which the poet claims as a truly feminine attribute.

The next nimphall involves two swains, Lalus and Cleon, who court the nymph Lirope with a progression of gifts. Lalus, a shepherd from the valley, offers her a lamb; but Cleon, a mountaineer, tops this with "a kid as white as milk." Both end their offers with a brief refrain, "So thou'lt leave him and goe with me," which recalls Marlowe's passionate shepherd saying, "Come live with me and be my love." Lirope refuses them both for the time being, but reserves a later acceptance if the need arises. Up go the offerings; this time Lalus suggests two white sparrows and is countered by Cleon's pair of vari-colored doves. These the nymph refuses since sparrows "scratch and bite" and "tame pigeons else you know are plenty." Then the lovers become more extravagant; Lalus offers to deck her with multitudes of flowers while Cleon wishes to cover her with gems. Again she denies them, but this time she hates to do it since:

> All in flowers, all so sweet,
> From the Crown, beneath the Feet,
> Amber, Currall, Ivory, Pearl,
> If this cannot win a Gerl,
> Thers nothing can. . . .
>
> ll. 267-71

Overcome, Lalus then offers a barge of reeds and flowers pulled by swans; and Cleon, a chariot escorted by nymphs and pulled by ostriches. Lirope indignantly spurns them now because of their excess in offering what was beyond them.

In the third nimphall a group of shepherds and nymphs gather together to celebrate the feast of Apollo. This nimphall is in three parts: a madding bout, Florimel's song, and a stately hymn to the Muses. The whole nimphall is actually an analysis of good poetry. In the madding bout the two swains, Doron and Dorilus, recite wildly and extravagantly while the two nymphs, Naiis and Cloe, recite clichés with excessive rhyme. Then in Florimel's song there is no beginning, middle, end, or subject. In these cases the principles of good poetry are taught by their absence. The men lack proper control over their inspiration; the nymphs lack that inspiration which gives originality to a creation; and Florimel lacks proper form. Finally the assembly of Elizium sings a hymn to the Muses. In this each of the muses is invoked and her powers are extolled. The hymn is the example of proper decorum and becomes a perfect contrast to the imperfect poetry which preceded it.

In the fourth nimphall Cloris tells of the shameful habits of dress and fashion existing among the women of Felicia (England). Satirically the nymphs condemn the court extravagances in the use of false hair, puffed sleeves, and tight apparel. After this ridicule of Felicia, Mertilla tells how she can face death because the other nymphs will carry on the ideals of Elizium.

In the fifth nimphall the aged hermit Clarinax welcomes the nymphs, Claia and Lelipa, as they gather flowers and herbs. The major theme in this section is the listing of several catalogs. First a group of boughs and sprays is given and connected with their classical function in a lament for the past; Claia then lists the flowers she will have for her garland; Lelipa follows this with her catalog of herbs she may wear; Clarinax then enumerates the simples with medicinal powers. But at the end they are grieved that their medicines will not help cure the evils of Felicia.

In the sixth nimphall a woodman, a fisher, and a shepherd each describe their occupation to prove that it is closest to the ideal. As these expositions are given in the hexameter of the *Poly-Olbion* (1612, 1622), the reader feels a closer connection here with the men who gave England her strength. Their descriptions are filled with highly realistic details taken from a close observation of nature. Although momentarily swayed in favor of the shepherd, the nymphs finally declare the debate won equally and crown them each with laurels.

Erotic love in the persons of Venus and Cupid are denied entrance to Elizium in the seventh nimphall. The introduction of fleshly passion would cause mischief in Elizium and disturb its tranquillity. Venus and Cupid try to enter Elizium in various disguises, and three nymphs and a boatman tell of how they discovered them. Finally Lelipa issues a mock proclamation in which she treats the goddess and her son as runaway slaves and calls for their capture, imprisonment, and punishment.

The high point in the entire work comes in the eighth nimphall. Here we have the preparations for the wedding of the nymph Tita with a Fay. This nimphall stands along with *Nimphidia* as a prime example of Drayton's fairy poetry. In contradiction to the custom of the real world, the marriage is an ideal one; based upon name and family relationships, it is carefully and deliberately made. There is no thought of a marriage based on the kind of passion which Venus and Cupid might represent.

The emphasis is on ceremony and decoration. Thus the nuptial song leads only to the door of the wedding chamber; all comments about the nuptial couch are omitted. Again Drayton emphasized the diminutiveness and delicateness of the fairy dress and ornamentation. In their efforts to outdo the elfin world in beauty and grandeur, the nymphs take special care with the wedding gown:

> Of Pansie, Pink, and Primrose leaves,
> Most curiously laid on in Threaves:
> And all the embroidery to supply,
> Powdered with flowers of Rosemary:
> A trail about the skirt shall runn,
> The silke-worms finest, newly spunn:
> And every Seam the Nimphs shall sew
> With th'smallest of the Spinners clew:
> And having done their work, again
> These to the Church shall bear her Train:
> Which for our Tita we will make
> Of the cast slough of a Snake,
> Which quivering as the wind doth blow,
> The Sun shall it like the Tinsell show.
>
> ll. 69-82

The Muses sing a hymn to Apollo in the ninth nimphall. Similar to the Classical hymns of Ovid, Horace, and Lucan, it praises his power and makes reference to many of the persons and places in which Apollo was mythologically involved. Drayton added his own touch with a Homeric listing by the nymphs of the twenty-one gems to be offered to the god. With nineteen of them the gems' magical or medicinal powers are included.

In the last episode two of the nymphs are frightened by a satyr who is seeking refuge from Felicia in Elizium. He tells how the forest and groves of Felicia are being denuded by the iron-age which is now threatening the very future of Felicia. He predicts the evil end of his homeland and prays that it may be avoided. The nymphs out of pity finally grant him asylum in Elizium. The satyr here represents both satire and the ideals of poetry. Drayton equates here, as he did in the *Poly-Olbion*, the destruction of England's forest with her growing neglect of the ideals of antiquity.

The Muses Elizium is Drayton's most perfect work and the culmination of his pastoral career. He took the best elements from his earlier pastoral works and united them in this his masterpiece. In this way he retained the careful attention to setting which was the mainstay of *Endimion and Phoebe*. He drew the holiday mood from the ninth eclogue of 1606. He kept the grace and lightness of his lyrics in the *Eclogs*. His satire he found in *The Man in the Moon* and *The Shepheards Sirena*. The nymphs, satyrs, hermits, and the other men in the sixth nimphall peopled the forests in *Poly-Olbion*. And finally, the over-all delicacy had its forerunner in *Nimphidia*.

As a pastoralist Drayton began with close imitation of his masters. But as he continued to write and experiment in this genre, his poetic talent grew until he created new and original pastoral forms. And as with *Idea*, his pastorals changed from the style of the Elizabethans to the new styles of a new age.

CHAPTER 3

Historical Poetry

THROUGHOUT Elizabeth's long reign and especially near its end, the tide of English patriotic nationalism and pride surged higher and higher. Because of this, the literature of the times became increasingly more involved in tracing the historical patterns and glorifying the outstanding figures of English history. Thus we have the chronicles of Stow, Camden, Holinshed, and Hall, the drama of Marlowe and Shakespeare, and the long list of historical poems which found their inspiration and impetus in the many editions of *The Mirrour for Magistrates.*

This work ostensibly offered a guide to men in responsible position and enabled them to avoid errors which might damage their future fame and their country. Basically, the legends in the *Mirrour* tradition were concerned with political sin and religious morality. They depicted a cause and effect relationship in the recounting of historical facts, and on the basis of a Christian sense of sin, they showed how the judgment of God determined the end results of an action. These legends finally became a handbook for rulers, warning them of the errors of their predecessors.

This kind of literature had a long and honorable background. Boccaccio's *De Casibus Virorum Illustrium* and his *De Claris Mulieribus* established the popularity of the genre on the continent. In England Chaucer utilized the same principle in *The Monk's Tale* and *The Legend of Good Women.* And finally, Lydgate applied the genre to English historical figures. However, a major difference appeared in the type with the writing of *The Fall of Princes.* In the works of Boccaccio and Chaucer, men and women met their downfall through no particular fault of their own. The fall of these men and women was controlled completely by Fortune and her wheel. In the works of Lydgate and his followers the motivation for the downfall was changed. Now Christian morality entered the scene; moral weakness or the commission of a crime became the cause of the downfall. In this genre as accepted by Lydgate and continued by the *Mirrour* authors, certain factors became associated with the legend or "de casibus" tale. Usually it was encased in either a dream or vision as a frame with the spirit of the dead hero recounting the story of his downfall; then in the sixteenth century a freight of analogy, historical learning, and didactic orientation gave an air of authority to the story; and finally the Boethian concept of Fortune and her wheel was interwoven with Christian judgment and morality. This *Mirrour* poetry appealed to the patriotic and historical taste of the times, and not merely to the literary. It became a kind of applied poetry; philosophy, history, and moral judgments were forced together into a poetic mold. In itself it inaugurated the popularity of a great series of tragedies in narrative verse and in drama.[1] It branched out into the historical epic, and for a time became associated with the Ovidian or erotic strain.

Drayton followed the popularity of the legend in publishing four: *Gaveston* in 1593; *Matilda* within the same year; *Robert of Normandy* in 1596; and *Thomas Cromwell* in 1607. Also in a new variation on this genre he published *England's Heroicall Epistles* which told of the downfall of important English figures using the letter convention. On the broader scale of longer historical poems he published the *Mortimeriados* in 1596, which he rewrote as *The Barons Warres* in 1603. Twenty-four years later in 1627 Drayton published the last of his new historical narrative poems, *The Battaile of Agincourt* and *The Miseries of Queene Margarite*. In all of these works Drayton sought to bring further glory to England through his poetic muse.

I   Piers Gaveston, Earl of Cornwall:
His Life, Death, and Fortune

The legend of *Piers Gaveston* was the first and longest of Drayton's complaints. Piers's ghost tells how he was the first favorite of Edward II with whom he had had a perverse relation-

ship. Edward was completely infatuated with the young de-
bauched Piers. He heaped honor after honor upon him, even to
the extent of seizing Queen Isabelle's dower of Cornwall and
giving this Earldom to his favorite. When the King had to leave
England on diplomatic missions, he made the young Earl the
Lord Protector of the kingdom. The King continued to ignore
his responsibilities to the peers and people of his land, and spent
his time and energies in dalliance with his favorite. The English
barons finally rebelled against the dissolute influence of Cornwall upon the King, and three times they forced his temporary
banishment. The besotted King looted the treasury to bestow
largess upon Piers. Finally the Barons rose in total rebellion,
captured, and hanged Piers Gaveston.

The story is told by Piers's ghost who emphasizes his emotional
state and his love for the King. The two are treated as lovers, and
a long series of descriptions are given of the grief suffered by
the parted lovers and their final separation by death. The basic
theme of Drayton's complaint is a King's downfall caused by
illicit passion. Fortune here is not the medieval figure, but a
siren calling Piers to his downfall. Lust has become the main-
spring of the plot which rises and falls as the fortunes of Piers
wax and wane.

Drayton made two later major revisions of this poem, in 1596
and in 1619. In the first revision Drayton strengthened the moral
attitudes in the poem condemning this illicit love. In the second
revision he deemphasized the part the King played in this lustful
liaison. With this cutting down of the element of lustful love, the
poem took on more of the tone of the early legends with the doc-
trine of mutability playing a more important part. He cut out
passages which discredited the King, and also deleted his tribute
to Idea at the end. He cut down the sections of long descriptions
of Piers's charms from nine stanzas to three and the account of
the first exile from thirty-seven to twelve.

In the first edition whenever Drayton wished to emphasize an
emotional situation he piled simile upon simile. In his revisions
he excluded many of these florid comparisons, and eliminated
many of the mythological conceits and other ornamentation. In
the final version the action moves quickly to Piers's final downfall since the hampering descriptive passages were eliminated.

In his work on historical poetry of the Renaissance, Homer Nearing suggests that the revised legend of *Gaveston* was to *Rosamund*, in the genre of historical poetry, as Shakespeare's *Richard II* was to Marlowe's *Edward II*, in the genre of historical drama. "It is," he says, "the apotheosis of a conception already great."[2]

II Matilda. The Faire and Chaste Daughter
of The Lord Robert Fitzwater

The second of the legends had no real basis in history except in a comment by John Stow of the part which a Lord Fitzwater took in the rebellion against King John.[3] Matilda herself is not mentioned; she is a creation of Drayton's muse. Although this poem was closely related to Daniel's *Rosamund*, Drayton added a new element in this complaint—chastity. In *Matilda*, the maiden who meets her death rather than suffering dishonor as paramour to the King is an exemplar of English chastity. As Drayton tells us in the poem, he considered that her chastity was a fitter subject for poetry than the illicit love of a Rosamund.

In the story Matilda's ghost relates that she, a great beauty, happened to catch the roving eye of the King who immediately desired her as his mistress. He continually sought her out. Determined to preserve her virtue, she defied him and fled to a nunnery where she took refuge. Enraged the King drove her father into exile and sent a messenger to give her one last chance to accept his proposal. When she again refused, the messenger gave her poison with which she toasted the King, as Rosamund had done. In the revised version of the poem, the messenger murdered her by holding a narcotic to her nostrils.

Matilda followed the rhyme royal of *The Rape of Lucrece* just as *Gaveston* had the sixain of *Venus and Adonis*. Also as in *Gaveston*, Drayton made two major revisions of the poem in 1596 and 1619.

In 1593 the same style which had characterized *Gaveston* predominated. Just like the first edition of his sonnet sequence *Matilda* was filled with heavy similes and long and extravagant conceits in the Petrarchan manner. Like *Gaveston* and the sonnet sequence many of these elaborate techniques were omitted in the successive revisions, especially that of 1619. Thus the lament by

Fitzwater (lines 519-616), his rage against the King (960-1036), and the King's repentance at her death (1051-1106) were omitted. The invocations (15-28, 50-56) and many of the purely descriptive and topical passages (99-105, 113-33, 334-50, 379-92; 36-42, 56-70, 1115-34) were also cut in the final revision.

In his final revision of 1619 Drayton made a better use of direct and dramatic action. In the original version a messenger had brought a letter to the nunnery in which King John made his final proposal. Matilda read it and soliloquized for over twenty-four stanzas before the poison began to affect her; however, in the last version the messenger carries no letter but has a quick and direct conversation with her. This makes the action pass more quickly in a more vital way.

Another of the techniques common to both *Matilda* and *Gaveston* in all editions was Drayton's use of aphorisms and *sententiae*, techniques in general use in the *Mirrour* legends. Thus in 1593 in a passage later dropped she discusses the duties of a King:

> "Kings be the Gods Vizegerents here on earth,
> "The Gods have power, Kings from that power have might,
> "Kings should excel in virtue as in birth,
> "Gods punish wrongs, & Kings should maintain right,
> "They be the Suns from which we borrow light.
>   "And they as Kings, should still in justice strive,
>   "With Gods, from whom their beings they derive."
>
>   ll. 827-34

In another passage which appears in all editions and which also illustrates the improvement in his syntax giving a more direct effect, these metaphoric aphorisms appear:

1593

> "The Lechers tongue is never void of guile,
> "Nor Crocodile wants tears to win his prey,
> "The subtil'st Temptor hath the sweetest style,
> "With rarest music Syrens soon'st betray.
> "Affection, will like fire himself bewray.
>   "Time offers still each hour to do amiss,
>   "And greatest dangers, promise greatest bliss."
>
>   ll. 239-45

1619

"The Lechers Tongue is never void of guile,
"Now wants he Tears, when he would win his prey,
"The subtilist Tempter hath the smoothest style,
"Syrens sing sweetliest when they would betray:
"Lust of itself hath never any stay,
    "Nor to contain it, bounds could have devised,
    "But most when fild, is least of all suffic'd."

ll. 169-75

The major ornamentation of the poem, as in *Gaveston,* is simile.
In this example from 1619 Matilda is plagued by the importun-
ings of the King:

When like a deer, before the Hounds imbost,
When him his strength beginneth to forsake,
Leaves the smooth Lands to which he trusted most,
And to the Covert doth himself betake
Doubling, and creeps from Brake again to Brake,
    Thus still I shift me from the Princes Face,
    Who had me then continually in Chase.

ll. 386-92

Instead of the long and violent repentance of the King which
drags out the early version, her death in 1619 is simply noted
with a few stanzas showing her virtue rewarded by Fame. One
of the best stanzas is this simile describing her death:

Thus like a Rose by some unkindly blast,
'Mongst many Buds, that round about it grow,
The with'ring leaves improsp'rously doth cast,
Whilst all the rest, their soverain Beauties show:
Amidst this goodly Sister-hood even so,
    Nipt with cold Death, untimely did I fade,
    Whilst they about me, pittious wailing made.

ll. 603-09

Basically this poem contains little real character analysis.
Matilda's ghost is too busy with self-complacent moralizing about
her virtue and laying claim to the title of an English Lucrece.
But in spite of its defects the story of Matilda was popular.
Anthony Mundy adapted Drayton's poem for the stage in *The*

Death in 1594, and Davenport repeated the story in another play *King John and Matilda*, thirty years later. Drayton himself adapted the story for his *England's Heroical Epistles* in 1597.

III   The Tragicall Legend of Robert, Duke of Normandy

The legend of *Robert* has the closest resemblance to the traditional *Mirrour* tales, for Drayton had replaced the theme of Eros with that of Fortune. In it the ghost of Robert never speaks; instead the poem consists of a debate between Fortune and Fame with the interstices filled with lush descriptions. The poem opens on the traditional dewy fresh morning, and then a long description is given of the landscape and the figures of the two goddesses who accompany Robert. Finally Fortune speaks and for seventeen stanzas she describes her powers. Fame then answers her and describes her powers and habitation. The House of Fame has a distinct resemblance to that which Chaucer had pictured over two centuries before:

> My dwelling place betwixt the earth and skies,
> My Turret unto heaven her top uprears,
> The windowes made of Lynceus piercing eyes,
> And all the walls be made of daintiest ears,
> Where every thing that's done in earth appears;
> No word is whispered in this vaulty round,
> But in my Palace straightways it doth sound.
>
> The pavement is of ratling brasen drums,
> The Rafters trumpets which do rend the air,
> Sounding aloud each name that thither comes,
> The chinks like tongues of all things talking there,
> And all things past, in memory do bear:
> The doors unlock with every word man saith,
> And open wide with every little breath.
>
> It's hung about with Arms and conquering spoils,
> The pillers which support the roof of this,
> Are trophies, graven with Herculean toils,
> The roof of garlands, crowns, and ensigns is,
> In midst of which a christall Pyramis:
> All over carv'd with men of most renown,
> Whose base is my fair chair, the spire my crown.
>
> (1596), ll. 344-64

When Fame has finished her denunciation of Fortune and her praise of herself, Fortune then tells the story of Robert and what she has done for him. Duke Robert was the eldest son of William the Conqueror. After William had successfully invaded England, Robert revolted against him and seized Normandy. Because of this William disinherited him and left the English throne to his second son, William Rufus. Robert then invaded England and forced Rufus to swear fealty to him and to pay an annual tribute. After this success Robert joined the Crusades and helped Godfrey capture Jerusalem. While Robert was enjoying good fortune in the Near East, William Rufus was assassinated and was succeeded by their younger brother Henry I. Upon Robert's return from the Crusades, he became embroiled in a dispute over the nonpayment of the tribute which Rufus had promised. The two brothers met in battle in Normandy, and the wheel of fortune turned for Robert. He was taken prisoner by Henry. When he attempted to escape, Henry had him blinded. (This detail was not mentioned by any of the chroniclers whom Drayton used as sources.)[4]

> But that he robb'd Duke Robert of his Sight,
> To turn the little piece of Day to Night,
>   As though that Sense, whose want should be the last
>   To all things living, he the first to taste.
>   (1619), ll. 620-23

Fortune then gives a résumé of her part in Robert's life and concludes with these words:

> Him I forbade, that any foe should kill
> Nor by his own hand suffred him to die,
> That life to Robert should be lothsome still,
> And that death from him evermore should fly,
> Making them both to him an enemy,
>   Willing to die, by life him double-killing,
>   Urged to live, twice dying, he unwilling.
>
> So many years as he had worn a Crown,
> So many years as he had hop'd to rise,
> So many years upon him did I frown,
> So many years he liv'd without his eyes,
> So many years in dying, ere he dies,
>   So many years shut up in prison strong;
>   'Though Sorrow make the shortest time seem long.

> Thus sway I in the course of Earthly things,
> To make Time work him everlasting spight,
> To shew how I can tyrannize on Kings,
> And in the fall of Great ones do delight,
> In fyned Things my working infinite:
>   All Worldly changes, at my will disposed,
>   For that in me all Wonder is inclosed.
>   (1619), ll. 638-58

Fame then tells her version of the story showing her influence upon Robert. She praises his knightly demeanor and prowess, and his service in the Crusades, which will bring him lasting glory. In an aside she rebukes Tasso for his failure to praise Robert in *Jerusalem Delivered* (1619; ll. 792-98). Fame vanquishes Fortune in the debate and announces that Robert's glory will last. Drayton ends the poem with a touch of sly humor:

> When gracefull Fame, convaying thence her charge,
> (As first with him, she thither did resort,)
> Gave me this Book, wherein was writ at large,
> His life, set out, though in this Legend short,
> T'amaze the World, with this so true report:
>   But Fortune, angrie with her Foe, therefore
>   Gave me the gift that I should still be poor.
>   (1619), ll. 939-45

The first edition of *Robert* appeared in 1596 written in 203 rhyme royal stanzas. Nine years later Drayton issued a revised edition which cut its length to 135; he reworked the poem again in 1619 primarily to smooth the syntax. The revisions follow the same basic pattern of his revisions of the other legends. He continued to drop the conceits, paradoxes, and long descriptions; he sought rhetorical simplification; and he strengthened his poem by adding more historical facts and eliminating some of the moralizing done by Fame and Fortune.

IV The Legend of Great Cromwell

This last of Drayton's legends was published in 1607 and was chosen for inclusion in the definitive edition of *The Mirrour for Magistrates* in 1610.[5] With the writing of this poem, Drayton returned completely to the traditional "de casibus" story of man's sudden downfall through the turn of Fortune's wheel. In this legend, Thomas Cromwell's ghost tells his own history. He re-

lates his humble origins and traces his rise to greatness. Early
in his career he served as an agent in Europe for English merchants, and upon his return to England he attached himself to
the service of Cardinal Wolsey. When the Cardinal fell from
favor, Cromwell transferred his loyalty to the King. He was especially useful to Henry VIII for his work in the dissolution of the
monasteries. Cromwell tells of the many honors which the King
heaped upon him:

> For first from Knighthood rising in degree,
> The office of Jewell-house my lot,
> After the Rolles he frankly gave to me,
> From whence a Privie Counseller I got,
> Then of the Garter: and then an Earl to be
> of Essex: yet sufficient these were not,
>> But to the great Viceregencie I grew,
>> Being a title as Supreme as New.

ll. 505-12

Cromwell relates the story of Francis Friscobald as an example
of the turning wheel of fortune. When Cromwell had been the
merchants' agent, the rich and influential Friscobald had aided
him; but now that the fortunes of the Englishman had risen,
those of the Florentine had fallen. Cromwell also relates the
vision of Pierce the Plowman on the evils of the popish church
and the seven deadly sins. Finally he reports how the marriage
he had made for the King with the Duchess of Cleves had been
the cause of his downfall. As the King dissolved the marriage,
Fortune looked away from the Earl. This was the end for him;
Fortune's wheel had turned. Nevertheless, Cromwell ends his
story with a boast:

> The Councell Chamber place of my arrest,
> Where chief I was, when greatest was the store,
> And had my speeches noted of the best,
> That did them high Oracles adore:
> A Parliament was lastly my Enquest,
> That was myself a Parliament before,
>> The Tower-hill Scaffold last did I ascend:
>> The Great'st Man of England made his end.

ll. 961-68

Cromwell was written in 121 *ottava rima* stanzas, and unlike
the other legends underwent few changes in the later editions.

The only changes were improvements in the rhetoric to make the language and rhythm flow more smoothly and evenly. The sources for this poem were Foxe's *Acts and Monuments,* and a play published by W. S. in 1602, *The True Chronicle History of the whole life and death of Thomas Lord Cromwell.* The story of Friscobald comes also from Bandello's *Novelle,* as well as Foxe and W. S. The section of the poem which gives the vision of Piers is a resume of Passus XX in the "B" text of Langland's *Pierce the Plowman.*[6]

In this legend Drayton attempted to give a fuller analysis of character than in any other of his poems. But its real value lies in the poet's understanding and perception of the forces of history, and in particular of the Reformation. Although Drayton definitely showed his anti-papist bias, he does see the Reformation as a problem of complexity. In his version he dropped much of the bitter vehemence against Rome which was the hallmark of Foxe's work; rather, the dominant note on the Reformation in Drayton's poem is a sorrow at the destruction of so much of England's treasures. The Cromwell story is simply told. There are no long bursts of rhetoric and description as are found in the earlier legends; his emphasis on Cromwell seems to be as an English Machiavelli.

V Mortimeriados (*1596*); The Barons Warres (*1603*)

Mortimeriados and *The Barons Warres* represent two Drayton versions of the same event. *Mortimeriados* was the first of Drayton's long narrative poems on the English wars of rebellion which occurred in the early fourteenth century. Then in 1603 Drayton issued *The Barons Warres* which changed the rhyme royal of the earlier version into ottava rima. Perhaps a major cause for this change was the fact that Samuel Daniel had written his *Civile Wars* (1595) in ottava rima. Tillotson maintained that "many of the changes made by Drayton in *The Barons Warres* might be summed up as an attempt to write a poem more like Daniel's: that is, a poem more historical, more critical, less romantic, less decorated" than the earlier *Mortimeriados.*[7]

In general *Mortimeriados* can be said to be closer in spirit to the Ovidian vein of the early *Gaveston,* while *The Barons Warres* is closer to the historical spirit of Daniel's work. Thus, in 1596

Drayton wrote a romance of passion; whereas, in 1603 he stressed the evils of civil dissension. The material in these two narrative poems has to do with the history of England from 1321 to 1330. Edward II was the King of England and Isabelle his Queen. He was a poor King who was held captive by an unnatural affection for his favorite, Hugh Dispenser, who had replaced the dead Gaveston. The English Barons, led by Roger Mortimer and his uncle, the Earl of March, had tried to protect their lands and prerogatives by rising in rebellion to force the King to dismiss the much hated favorite. The Barons lost, and the Mortimers were thrown into the Tower of London. Through the connivance of the Queen and the Bishop of Hereford, Roger escaped the tower and fled to France. Soon afterwards, the Queen herself left on an embassy to France where she took young Mortimer as her lover. Then by trickery she managed to have her son Edward, the heir apparent, also sent to France. When the prince arrived, he joined with his mother and Mortimer in a plot to overthrow his father the King. Assisted by the French, the Queen's forces seized England, forced the King to abdicate, then imprisoned him.

Finally, with the help of the Bishop of Hereford, the Queen and Mortimer arranged the death of her husband by means of an ambiguous note to his jailers. *"Edwardum occidere nolite timere bonum est."* If a comma were placed after *nolite*, the translation read: "Do not kill Edward, it is a good thing to fear." However if the comma were seen after *timere*, the meaning changed to: "Do not fear to kill Edward, it is a good thing." The comma was omitted, and the jailers knew well where the Queen would have had it. After this murder of the deposed King, Mortimer was created Earl of March, and ruled England together with the Queen who was regent for her minor son, Edward III. Eventually Mortimer's ambitions grew too strong, and the young Edward III ordered him executed. The sixth and last canto ends with Queen Isabelle mourning the death of her lover.

The Barons Warres is filled with long similes and descriptions which lend color to the narrative, rather than overpowering it as in *Mortimeriados*. For instance, in Canto VI of the latter poem, Drayton uses one stanza to describe the excessive pride of Queen Isabelle and Mortimer, and then used the next three stanzas to enlarge upon the previous description.

When Drayton holds to the action in his narrative, the pace picks up as he employs a more direct style. The death of Edward II in Canto V is illustrative of his vivid narrative:

> When 'twixt Two beds they clos'd his wearied Coarse,
> Basely uncovering his most secret part,
> And without Humane Pity, or Remorse,
> With a hot Spit they thrust him to the Heart.
> O that my pen had in it but that force,
> T'expresse the Pain! but that surpasseth Art;
>   And that, the Soul must even with trembling do,
>   For words want weight, nor can they reach thereto.
>
> When those (i' th' depth and dead time of the Night)
> Poor simple People, that then dwelled near,
> Whom that strange noise did wond'rously affright,
> That his last Shriek did in his parting hear,
> As pittying that most miserable Wight,
> (Betwixt Compassion and obedient Fear)
>   Turned up their Eyes, with Heaviness opprest,
>   Praying to Heaven, to give the Soul good rest.
>   *BW* V; ll. 513-28

The poem is filled with classical allusions, although again a great number had been deleted in the revision. Thus, when Mortimer's tower is described, it takes fourteen eight-line stanzas to describe the classical paintings on the wall of the lover's bower: Phoebus clipping Hyacynth's hair; "Apollo's Quiver, a farre-killing Bow"; "Ne'r that was Io, in a Heyfer's shape"; "There Mercurie was like a Shepheards Boy/Sporting with Hebe"; "By them in Landship, rocky Cynthus reared"; "The half naked nymphs, some climbing, some descending"; "In one part, Phaeton cast among the clouds/By Phoebus Palfreys" (*BW*, VI, ll. 257-328). And then comes a detailed description of the bed and its covering:

> In part of which, under a golden vine,
> Which held a curious Canopy through all
> Stood a rich Bed, quite cover'd with the twyne,
> Shadowing the same, in the redoubling fall,
> Whose clusters drew the branches to decline,
> 'Mongst which, did many a naked CUPID sprawl:
>   Some, at the sundry-cloured Birds did shoot,
>   And some, about to pluck the Purple Fruit.

On which, a Tissue counterpayne was cast,
Arachnes Web did not the same surpass,
Wherein the stories of his fortunes past,
In lively Pictures, neatly handled was;
How he escap'd the Tower, in France how grac'd
With stones imbroyd'red, of a wond'rous Mass;
About the Border, in a fine-wrought Fret,
Emblem's, Empressa's, Hieroglyphicks set.

BW VI; ll. 329-44

Mortimer and Edward both appear as firmly shaped tragic figures. Edward is deposed because of his moral frailty and intemperate will; Mortimer is destroyed because of his excessive pride and overweening ambition. However, in the revision Edward is shown in the best possible light since Drayton then desired to emphasize not the moral evils of the King's lapse, but rather those evils which are attendant upon a civil conflict. Also as in Canto V, stanza 15-17, Drayton is stressing the sanctity of kingship.

In *The Barons Warres* Drayton dropped much of the romantic story and ornamentation as he had done in his revisions of the legends. In his new version he added such epic devices as invocations, apostrophes to Providence, Fate, and the Muses, and heroic catalogs of the warriors shire by shire (c.II, st.22-26) and of the Queen's commanders (c.IV, st.16).

These two poems are extensions of the "de casibus" tale with additional details prompted by the intense popularity of works dealing with English history. Other works which followed this same trend of expansion of the legend were Thomas Storer's *The Life and Death of Thomas Cardinal Wolsey* in 1599, Sir Francis Hubert's *The Historie of Edward II* about 1609, Christopher Brook's *The Ghost of Richard III* in 1614, and Patrick Gordon's *The Famous Historie of the Renowned and Valiant Robert Surnamed the Bruce* in 1615.

VI   The Battaile of Agincourt *and* The Miseries of Queene Margarite

In 1627 Drayton published the last of his narrative historical poems. Both *The Battaile of Agincourt* and *The Miseries of Queene Margarite* proceeded from the same source of historical interest which was a motivating factor in the writing of *The*

Barons Warres. Both of the new poems were written in ottava rima with the former having 315 stanzas and the latter 257.

In *The Battaile of Agincourt* Drayton departed from his previous technique of having a person as the focal point of his historical poems. Of course Henry plays a major role, but the poem is not about him. In *Battaile* Drayton was celebrating a major event in English history. The purpose of the poem was at once didactic and nationalistic. He divided the work into two parts: the preparation for the great battle and the battle itself. In keeping with his own consideration of this as a short epic poem, he includes all of the trappings of the epic. The appropriate invocations are present, and the speeches by the English and French leaders are most effective. Drayton sprinkles his poem with many catalogs and lists which give the reader a broad panoramic effect.[8]

When Drayton desired to impress the reader with the horrors of war, he gave short specific instances of bloodshed which easily captured the effect he sought. An example of this is found in his description of the siege at Harfleur:

> An old man sitting by the fire side,
> Decrepit with extremity of Age,
> Stilling his little Grand-child when it cried,
> Almost distracted with the Batteries rage:
> Sometimes doth speak it fair, sometimes doth chide,
> As thus he seeks its mourning to assuage,
> > By chance a Bullet doth the chimney hit,
> > Which falling in, doth kill both him and it.
>
> Whilst the sad weeping Mother sits her down,
> To give her little new-born Babe the Pap:
> A luckless quarry leveld at the Town,
> Kills the sweet Baby sleeping in her lap,
> That with the fright she falls into a swoon,
> From which awak'd, and mad with the mishap;
> > As up a Rampire shrieking she doth clim,
> > Comes a great Shot, and strikes her lim from lim.
>
> ll. 785-800

Although Drayton held close to his chronicle sources of Raphael Holinshed and John Speed, the resultant poem became a dramatic depiction of the events. Another technique Drayton continually employed in his historical works after 1596 was the extensive use of marginal notes with which he explained any passage or reference which might be beyond the scope of the reader. These notes were completely in keeping with Drayton's concept of poetry proceeding out of learning.

In general Drayton managed to capture the same heroic spirit which had dominated his "Ballad of Agincourt." As a narrative poem *The Battaile of Agincourt* is far superior to his early work, and will amply repay the reader's efforts with an abundance of pleasure.

In *The Miseries of Queene Margarite* Drayton once again drew upon the chronicles of Holinshed and Hall. However, in this case he failed to depart sufficiently from his sources. There are no truly dramatic incidents as in *Battaile* and the other earlier historical narrative poems. In fact *Miseries* is, as Nearing states, "a bone-dry chronicle in verse."[9]

Drayton tried to apply the analytic treatment of Cromwell to the character of Margarite, but somehow she never emerges as the chief figure within the poem. The major focus does not fall upon her, but upon the whole group of major figures in the early part of the War of the Roses: Henry VI, Suffolk, Somerset, Warwick, and Edward IV. Because of this diffusion, the poem seems to lack any real unity. Drayton did not have his poetic fancy engaged by anyone in the poem. He rather seems to have merely recorded some political history during the War of the Roses. As far as the love story between Queen Margarite and Suffolk is concerned, Drayton had done a much better job in their exchange of letters in *England's Heroicall Epistles.*

This poem is not one of Drayton's better efforts. However, in all fairness it must be pointed out that there are certain excellent passages in the poem. When Drayton stopped his chronicling long enough to describe the landscape or make an observation on an event, the resultant lines become well worth reading. Thus this short passage on the battle at Blore-Heath gives the real tragedy of civil war:

> This fire in ev'ry family thus set,
> Out go the Brown Bills, with the well-strung Bows,
> Till at Blore-heath these boistrous soldiers met,
> For there it chanc'd the Armies then to close,
> This must not live, if that he strove to let;
> Never such friends yet ere became such Foes,
>   With down-right strokes they at each other lay,
>   No word for Cheshire was, but kill, and slay.

> The Son (as some report) the Father slew
> In opposition as they stoutly stood,
> The Nephew seen the Unkle to pursue,
> Bathing his sword in his own natural blood:
> The Brother in his Brothers gore imbrew
> His guilty hands, and at this deadly food:
> > Kinsman kills kinsman, which together fall,
> > As hellish fury had possest them all.
>
> > > ll. 745-60

It is in several scattered passages such as this one that flashes of real poetry are contained. However, the poem as a whole lacks vividness, and is not one of Drayton's better historical poems.

VII   Englands Heroicall Epistles

The most lastingly popular of Drayton's historical poetry was his *Englands Heroicall Epistles*. The first eighteen were published in 1597; five more were added the next year; and the last was included in 1599 to make a total of twenty-four epistles. These poems were part of Drayton's real contributions to English poetry. He went back to the classical period and took the form and idea from Ovid's *Heroides*. This was not the first time that the Ovidian love letter had been seen in English literature. Chaucer and Gower had used the material from the *Heroides* in their verse, but they had not used the letter form. In 1567 George Turberville had translated the Roman poet in *The Heroycal Epistles of the Learned Publius Ovidius Naso in English Verse . . . with Aulus Sabinus Answers to the Same*. It was left to Drayton to return to the actual letter form and to introduce characters from English history as the correspondents. In this way Drayton continued to follow the patriotic trend he established in his other historical poetry.

The Heroicall Epistles was closely associated with the legends of the *Mirrour* tradition and the popular historical drama of the period. However, the epistles are not true narratives; they do not tell a full story. Rather they are segments taken out of a known historical action, which represent an emotional high point in the lives and loves of the various characters. It is actually this fact which makes the letters so excellent. In each case the writer had a real reason and occasion to write about his or her emotional crisis with a probable expectation of receiving an answer.

Since the readers were well aware of the history which surrounded each of the ostensible letter writers, they were better able to savor the emotions, passions, expectations, and frustrations which the several letters expressed. With the exception of the Matilda and King John exchange, which Drayton had already written of in his legend, all of the stories were found in contemporary literature. At least five of the twelve stories were told in *The Mirrour for Magistrates*. Other sources which made these stories familiar to the Elizabethans were William Warner's *Albion's England*, Daniel's *The Complaint of Rosamund* and *The Civile Wars*, Thomas Churchyard's and Anthony Chute's versions of *Shore's Wife*, Marlowe's *Edward II*, Shakespeare's *Richard II* and *Henry VI*, and Thomas Nashe's *Unfortunate Traveller*. Aside from these Drayton himself gives us some of the sources he used in writing these epistles. In the *Annotations* which followed each letter in the early editions of the poems, Drayton mentioned such sources as Jean Froissart, Polydore Vergil, Edward Hall, John Foxe, John Stow, and William Camden.

Drayton arranged these twelve pairs of letters in chronological order from the first exchange of Rosamund and King Henry II in the late twelfth century to the final exchange of Lady Jane Gray and Dudley in 1553. And as the series progresses, references are made to earlier stories and loves. Thus, Matilda in the second pair reminds King John of the fate of Rosamund of the first; Alice of Salisbury writes to the Black Prince and mentions both Matilda and Rosamund; and in the last pair Lady Jane Gray and Dudley refer to the Mary Tudor and Charles Brandon episode.

Drayton managed to achieve variety in the letters according to their content and the expected outcome as contrasted with what the reader frequently knew to be the actual fate of the writer. With this as a basis, Drayton's letters can be generally grouped in different sets. In the first group are Edward the Black Prince and Alice Countess of Salisbury; Queen Katharine and Owen Tudor; and Mary Tudor of France and Charles Brandon Duke of Suffolk. In these there is a proposal of marriage and its acceptance, and the reader is aware of the happy ending of the love stories. On the other hand in the Henry Howard Earl of Surrey and Lady Geraldine exchange the happiness which the writers anticipate is dramatic irony to the reader who is aware of the ultimate disaster of the beheading of the Earl. In the third group which consists of Elinor Cobham and Duke Humphrey, Queen Isabel and Richard II, and Lady Jane Gray and Gilford Dudley, tragedy has already struck one of the writers and the reader can sympathize with them as they look forward to their ultimate misfortune. The common factor in Rosamund and King Henry II, Edward IV and Mistress Shore, and King John and Matilda is that each of the ladies concerned is the object of royal attention which ultimately will cause her death. And finally in the exchanges between Queen Isabel and Mortimer, and Queen Margaret and William de-la-Poole, Duke of Suffolk, the close approximation to the love in the *Heroides* is dampened for the reader by the knowledge of the approaching execution of Mortimer and Suffolk, of which the supposed authors of the letters are unaware.

In this way Drayton achieved a variety of sentiments all grouped around the central theme of love. By choosing such high points of emotion and passion in the lives of the writers Drayton expressed a deep psychological insight into the human heart. It was this approach together with his use of the heroic couplet which made these poems so popular through the eighteenth century.

As a craftsman Drayton outdid himself in this work in comparison with the other poems he had written to this time. Although he used the mythological allusions and decorations common to his early work, he nevertheless used them sparingly and with restraint. We have seen how Drayton was really his own best critic as he continually revised and improved his works. But he seemed to be satisfied with *Englands Heroicall Epistles*. With the exception of some pruning here and there to eliminate a few diffuse and repetitive passages, Drayton made no major revisions in his letter poems.

It is interesting to note that as Daniel and Lodge had placed their complaints of *Rosamund* and *Elstred* next to their sonnet cycles of *Delia* and *Licia* in their published form, Drayton chose *Englands Heroicall Epistles* rather than one of his legends such as *Matilda* to be the companion piece of his sonnet sequence *Idea* in 1599 and in later editions.

Drayton mingled many different styles in this work. In the

Rosamund and King John exchange the strong rhetorical and declamatory style echoes the style of Ovid's own work in Latin in the *Heroides*. Whereas in the Surrey letter to Geraldine there are descriptive passages closely allied to his Petrarchan work:

> Near that fair Castle is a little Grove,
> With hanging Rocks all cover'd from above,
> Which on the Bank of goodly Thames doth stand,
> Clipt by the Water from the other Land,
> Whose bushy Top doth bid the Sun forbear,
> And checks his proud Beams, that would enter there;
> Whose Leaves still mutt'ring, as the Air doth breathe,
> With the sweet bubbling of the Stream beneath,
> Doth rock the Senses (whilst the small Birds sing)
> Lulled asleep with gentle murmuring;
> Where light-foot Fairies sport at Prison-Base,
> (No doubt there is some Pow'r frequents the place)
> There the soft Poplar and smooth Beech do bear
> Our Names together carved ev'rywhere,
> And Gordian Knots do curiously entwine
> The Names of Henry and Geraldine.
> O, let this Grove in happy times to come,
> Be call'd, The Lovers bless'd Elizium;
> Whither my Mistress wonted to resort,
> In Summers heat, in those sweet shades to sport:
> A thousand sundry Names I have it given,
> And call'd it, Wonder-hider, Cover-Heaven,
> The Roof where Beauty her rich Court doth keep
> Under whose compass all the starrs do sleep.
> There is one Tree, which now I call to mind,
> Doth bear these Verses carved in his Rind:
> When Geraldine shall sit in thy fair shade,
> Fan her sweet Tresses with perfumed Air,
> Let thy large boughs a Canopy be made,
> To keep the Sun from gazing on my Fair;
> And when thy spreading branched Arms be sunk,
> And thou no Sap nor Pith shalt more retain,
> Ev'n from the dust of thy unwieldy Trunk,
> I will renew thee Phoenix-like again,
> And from thy dry decayed Root will bring
> A new-born Stem, another Aesons Spring.

ll.191-226

The early metaphysical style can be seen in this passage which
Edward IV writes to Mistress Shore:

> Me thinks thy Husband takes his mark awry,
> To set his Plate to sale, when thou art by;
> When they which do thy Angel-locks behold,
> As the base Dross, do but respect his Gold,
> And wish one Hair, before that maddie Heap,
> And but one Lock, before the Wealth of Cheape:
> And for no cause else hold we Gold so dear,
> But that it is so like unto thy Hair.
> And sure I think, Shore cannot choose but flout
> Such as would find the great Elixar out,
> And laugh to see the Alchemists, that choke
> Themselves with Fumes, and waste their Wealth in Smoke;
> When if thy Hand but touch the grossest Mold,
> It is converted to refined Gold:
> When theirs is chaff'red at an easier rate,
> Well knowne to all, to be adulterate;
> And is no more, when it by thine is set,
> Then paltry Beugle, or light-prized Jet.

ll. 71-88

The epistles are filled with *sententiae*, epigrams, and pithy
antitheses which would eventually blossom in the developed
couplets of Dryden and Pope. W. J. Courthope wrote that "in
his terse epigrams and antitheses we have the germs of the style
which reached its last development in Pope's treatment of the
heroic couplet."[10] An examination of two of the twelve pairs of
the letters shows that 267 of the 345 couplets are fully closed,
making a percentage of over seventy-six. This was indeed a
higher rate than any other of the sixteenth-century poets who
used the couplet. Robert Hillyer and Mario Praz both agreed
that Drayton is to be given credit as the real pioneer in the use
of the closed heroic couplet. Hallet Smith felt that Drayton had
borrowed the couplet from Marlowe, but had also greatly developed it probably under the influence of the Latin distich of
Ovid.[11]

A few excerpts from *Englands Heroicall Epistles* will more
accurately give a reader the flavor of Drayton's couplets:

Is it a King the wofull Widdow hears?
Is it a King dryes up the Orphans Tears?
Is it a King regards the Clyents crie?
Gives Life to him, by Law condemn'd to die?
Is it his care the Common-wealth that keeps,
As doth the Nurse her Babie, whilst it sleeps?
And that poor King of all those Hopes prevented,
Unheard, unhelp'd, unpitti'd, unlamented?

"King John" ll. 55-62

Few be my words, but manifold my Woe,
And still I stay, the more I strive to goe.
Then till fair Time some greater Good affords,
Take my Loves-payment in these ayrie Words.

"Queen Isabel to Mortimer" ll. 161-64

Art thou offended, that thou are beloved?
Remove the cause, th'effect is soon remov'd;
Indent with Beautie how far to extend,
Set downe Desire a Limit where to end;
Then charm thine eyes, that they no more may wound,
And limit Love to keep within a Bound.
If thou do this, nay then thou shalt do more,
And bring to pass what never was before;
Make Anguish sportive, craving all Delight,
Mirth solemn, sullen, and inclin'd to Night,
Ambition lowly, Envie speaking well,
Love, his Relief, for Niggardize to sell.

"Edward the Black Prince" ll. 57-68

How shall I call my self, or by what Name
To make thee know from whence these letters came?
Not from thy Husband, for my hateful Life
Make thee a Widdow, being yet a wife:
Nor from a King; that Title I have lost,
Now of that Name, proud Bullenbrooke may boast:
What I have been, doth but this comfort bring,
No words so wofull, as, I was a King.

"Richard II" ll. 7-14

These are but a few gems from the letters. On every one of the one hundred and sixty pages of the Epistles are passages worth quoting to illustrate Drayton's smooth versification. Louis Wright gave a perfect description of this work when he wrote that in Drayton's epistles "the pure metal of history was mingled with a pleasing alloy of Romantic love story."[12]

CHAPTER 4

Poly-Olbion

IN 1594 Drayton published an Amour in *Ideas Mirrour* which described the beauties of England and which contained in essence the germ of his later *magnum opus*:

>Our floods-Queen Thames, for ships & Swans is crowned,
>   And stately Severn, for her shores is praised,
>   The Crystal Trent, for Fords & fish renowned,
>   And Avons fame, to Albyons Cliffs is raised.
>Carlegion Chester, vaunts her holy Dee,
>   Yoke, many wonders of her Ouse can tell,
>   The Peake her Dove, whose banks so fertile be,
>   And Kent will say, her Medway doth excell.
>Cotswoold commends her Isis and her Tame,
>   Our Northern borders boast of Tweeds fair flood,
>   Our Western parts extoll their Wilys fame,
>   And old Legea brags of Danish blood:
>Ardens sweet Ankor let they glory be,
>That fair Idea she doth live by thee.

By 1598 Drayton was hard at work on his major work, a fact Francis Meres reported in *Palladis Tamia*. Finally in 1612 the first eighteen songs appeared under the highly descriptive title: *Poly-Olbion. Or a Chorographicall Description of Tracts, Rivers, Mountaines, Forest, and other parts of this renowned Isle of Great Britaine, With intermixture of the most Remarkable Stories, Antiquities, Wonders, Rarityes, Pleasures, and Commodities of the same: Digested in a Poem by Michael Drayton, Esq. With a table added, for direction to those occurences of Story and Antiquity whereunto the Course of the Volume easily leades not.* Ten years later Drayton finished the remaining twelve songs which finished his poetical tour of England and Wales.

Poly-Olbion is an unusual poetical form. In it there is nothing really new, but the drawing together of several kinds of poetry within this one work makes it unique. Basically Drayton combined four diverse elements in this poem: geography; history, both real and legendary; allegorical representation; and the pastoral element. Each of these individual elements had long existed in poetry, and in some cases combinations of two of the elements had been used before as incidental elements in other poems. Thus in a minor way both Ovid in the *Metamorphoses* and Virgil in *The Aeneid* and *The Georgics* had combined literal topographical verse with mythological allusions and personifications of persons and things as incidental decorations.[1]

The combination of the topographical with allegorical representation was found throughout the Tudor pageants and masques. In these versified dramatic presentations the rivers and cities of England were personified and involved in amours with other *genii locorum*. Thus, in the masque, *The Rock Adamantine*, presented in honor of Queen Elizabeth at Gray's Inn in 1595, Proteus accompanied by tritons and sea nymphs is involved with the figures of Thamesis and Aphrodite. Also the masques of Ben Jonson, Samuel Daniel, and Francis Beaumont contain marriages of rivers, and stories of other amours of these allegorical personifications.[2]

Prior to Drayton, all of the poets who had written topographical poetry had done so on a relatively small scale. Generally their poems or plays were written for some other purpose and included the topographical element to describe a place or region, or even as a mere decoration. Drayton's work was a vast undertaking which endeavored to describe all of England and Wales. Instead of being a minor ingredient, the topographical element became the dominant one of the long poem.

Because of the overflow of nationalistic pride which characterized the English Renaissance, Drayton chose England as his background and described the many natural beauties of the country he loved. To this he added the great wealth of history and legend which formed an important part of the English heritage. His known abilities as a scholar enabled him to search out all of the historical background attendant upon all parts of England. His vast knowledge of the classics allowed him to draw appropriate comparisons between the glories of the classical

cultures and those of England, naturally to the latter's advantage.
Also he was able to interweave the Ovidian amours and classical
myths in his English landscape, and as pastoral poet Drayton
was able to incorporate the idyllic rural elements in this work.
As a keen observer of nature, he was able to list the homes and
habits of England's trees, birds, and fish. In this way the poet,
scholar, pastoralist, and nature observer combined disparate elements into a major poem which celebrated the glories of England and Wales. Drayton assembled all of the interests of the
earlier topographical poets, combined them with his own genius,
and then passed *Poly-Olbion* on to posterity as the final word in
this genre.

A meticulous craftsman, Drayton carefully examined and used
many sources in his composition of this fifteen-thousand line
poem. Primarily, his sources were William Camden's *Britannia,*
Holinshed's *Chronicles,* and Humphrey Llwyd's translation of
Caradoc of Llancarfan's *The Historie of Cambria.* Modern
scholars, especially J. William Hebel and Vernon Hull, have
thoroughly and carefully analyzed *Poly-Olbion* to determine the
many sources Drayton used in composing the individual songs.
Aside from the literary sources which he used in his writing,
Drayton also drew upon his own travels and the sights he had
personally seen to assist him in his descriptions. Thus his lines
on his home county Warwickshire, and on such dispersed areas
as Kent, Cornwall, Westmoreland, and Dorset form passages
which reflect his own lively appreciation of beauties noticed on
his travels.

The decided emphasis of the poem is on the rural aspect of
England and Wales. In "To the Generall Reader" of the first
part of *Poly-Olbion* Drayton gave us in his own words the image
he wished us to find in his work:

In such a season, when the idle humerous world must hear of nothing,
that either savors of Antiquity, or may awake it to seek after more,
then dull and slothfull ignorance may easily reach unto: These, I say,
make much against me; and especially in a Poem, from any example,
either of Ancient, or Modern, that have proved difficult, to the female
Sex, yea, and I fear, to some that think themselves not meanly learned,
being not rightly inspired by the Muses: such I mean, as had rather
read the fantasies of foreign inventions, than to see the Rarities and
History of their own Country delivered by a true native Muse. Then,

whosoever thou be, possest with such stupidity and dullness, that, rather than thou wilt take pains to search into ancient and noble things, choosest to remain in the thick fogs and mists of ignorance, as near the common Lay-stall of a city: refusing to walk forth into the *Tempe* and fields of the Muses, where through most delightful Groves and Angelic harmony of Birds shall steal thee to the top of an easy hill, where in artificial caves, cut out of the most natural Rock, thou shalt see the ancient people of this Isle delivered thee in their lively images: from whose height thou may behold both the old and later times, as in thy prospect, lying far under thee; then conveying thee downe by a soul-pleasing Descent through delicate embroidered Meadows, often veined with gentle gliding Brooks; in which thou may fully view the dainty Nymphs in their simple naked beauties, bathing them in crystalline streams; which shall lead thee, to most pleasant Downs, where harmless Shepherds are, some exercising their pipes, some singing roundelays, to their gazing flocks.

In this work Drayton's muse travels over the length and breadth of England and Wales. Each of the songs describes a specific area on her journey. She begins on the islands of the coast of Cornwall and makes her way along the southern coast to the Isle of Wight. She then turns north to the Bristol area and crosses the Severn to the Cardiff region. From here she travels to the west coast and up north to the Cardigan area. Next she turns her attention to the inland region of Wales, moving from the Hereford section north to Anglesey. After exploring the Mersey she wends her way inland in a southerly direction back to Hastings and then Dover. The second part of *Poly-Olbion* opens with the muse on the east coast just north of the Thames. She continues her journey northward around the Wash, from where she crosses northwest to Lancashire. Then she returns east to Yorkshire and proceeds north to Berwick. Lastly, she crosses west to the Lake District where she finishes her journey.

As the muse visits each of these regions, she tells of the history and legends associated with that particular region. Thus in the first song when the muse mentions Totnesse, she relates the story of the Trojans from Aeneas' flight until young Brutus set his foot on Albion's soil. In the seventeenth song she tells of the kings of England who had sailed upon the Thames from the Bastard William to Queen Elizabeth.

All of the legends and history of England are related in this poem to a particular place or region. By reading any one of the songs we receive a picture of a particular region which includes its topographical, historical, and legendary backgrounds.

Poly-Olbion has several elements giving a structural unity to the thirty songs. First of all the journey itself gives a coherence to the poem as the specific sequences of places visited are drawn together by the geographical affinity of England and Wales. Secondly, the constant presence of the peripatetic Muse gives cohesion throughout the poem. The continual desire for the pleasures of England's Golden Age is contrasted with the encroachment of modern ideas and inventions. And finally, Drayton's use of the device of contention strengthens the unity of the poem. Throughout the thirty songs there are various kinds of disputes: thus river fights river; mountains contend against plains; and man fights man. For instance, in the fourth song is the great debate between England and Wales over the ownership of the Isle of Lundy. Another major contention is between the glories of Albion and those of ancient Greece and Rome. This battle permeates the poem usually under the surface, but every so often it rises to the public view. Because of this implicit debate, the victory of the Britons over Rome is celebrated with gusto in the eighth song.

The ancient religion of the Druids is shown to be stronger and more virile than that of the Romans in the sixth song. And even the value of Lemster wool is priced far beyond that of the Golden Fleece:

> At Lemster, for her Wool whose staple doth excel,
> And seems to over-match the golden Phrydian Fell,
> Had this our Colchos been unto the Ancients known,
> When Honow was her self, and in her glory shown,
> He then that did command the Infantry of Greece,
> Had only to our Isle adventur'd for this Fleece.
> VII:145-50

The glory of Malvern Hill is maintained over that of Mount Olympus in lines 52-132 of the seventh song. And in a humorous vein Drayton sings that the stench of Holland Marsh takes the laurels away from the Acherusian Fen in this unwholesome category:

> From this our Southern part of Holland, call'd the Low,
> Where Crowland's ruins yet, (though almost buried) show
> How mighty Founders power, yet his more Christian zeal,
> She by the Muses aid, shall happily reveal
> Her sundry sorts of Fowl, from whose abundance she
> Above all other Tracts, may boast her self to be
> The Mistress, (and indeed) to sit without compare,
> And for no worthless soil, should in her glory share,
> From her moist seat of Flags, of Bulrushes and Reed,
> With her just proper praise, thus Holland doth proceed.
>   Yee Acherusian Fens, to mine resign your glory,
> Both that which lies within the goodly Territory
> Of Naples, as that Fen Thesposia's earth upon
> Whence that infernal Flood, the smutted Acheron
> Shoves forth her sullen head, as thou most fatall Fen,
> Of which Hetrurua tells, the wat'ry Thrasimen,
> In History although thou highly seemst to boast,
> That Haniball by thee o'rthrew the Roman Host.
> I scorn th' Egyptian Fen, which Alexandria shows,
> Proud Mareotis, should my mightiness oppose,
> Or Scythia, on whose face the Sun doth hardly shine,
> Should her Meotis think to match with this of mine,
> That covered all with Snow continually doth stand.
> I stinking Lerna hate, and the poore Libian Sand.
>
> XXV:21-44

Indeed, England is peopled with more fairies and gods than even the most ancient haven for divinities. In fact, at the report of England's Fame, Neptune himself abandoned his classic home in the southern climes:

> But, partly by the floods sent hither from the shore,
> As one among the rest, a brave and lusty Dame
> Call'd Portsey, when that Bay of Portsmouth hath her name:
> By her, two little Isles, her handmaids (which compar'd)
> With those within the Poole, for defness not out-dar'd)
> The greater Haling hight: and fairest though by much,
> Yet Thorney very well, but some-what rough in touch.
> Whose beauties far and near divulged by report,
> And by the Trytons told in mighty Neptune's Court,

> Old Proteus hath been known to leave his finny herd,
> And in their sight to sponge his foam-bespawled beard.
> The Sea-gods, which about the wat'ry kingdom keep,
> Have often for their sakes abandoned the Deep;
> That Thetis many a time to Neptune hath complaind,
> How for those wanton Nymphs her Ladies were disdain'd:
> And there rose such rut th' unruly rout among,
> That soone the noise thereof through all the Ocean rung.
>
> ll. 429-46

Another unifying element is the presence of the constant pride in all things English. In his address to the reader which was quoted above, Drayton castigated those who sought "foreign inventions" and ignored the "true native Muse." In the preface to the second part in 1622 he again made an appeal to the patriotic sentiments of the readers he had hoped to gain:

First, that it was a new clear way, never before gone by any; then that it contained all the Delicacies, Delights, and Rarities of this renowned Isle, interwoven with the Histories of the Britanes, Saxons, Normans, and the later English: And further that there is scarcely any of the Nobility, or Gentry of this land, but that he is some way or other, by his Blood interested therein.

As previously stated, one of the dominant themes in the poem is the nostalgic desire for a return to England's Golden Age together with a hatred for the encroachments of the dissolute Jacobean era. In this first sense *Poly-Olbion* has much of the same spirit as Spenser's *The Ruins of Time*. The poet says that what has passed was good, but today things are getting bad, and tomorrow they will be worse. For instance, Drayton wrote of the Christianizing of the fierce Saxons, then he broke off to excoriate the evils of the new times:

> A people from their first bent naturally to spoil,
> That cruelty with them from their beginning brought.
> Yet when the Christian faith in them had throughly wrought,
> Of any in the world no story shall us tell,
> Which did the Saxon race in pious deeds excell:
> That in these drowsy times should I in public bring
> Each great peculiar Act of every godly King,

The world might stand amazed in this our Age to see
Those goodly Fanes of theirs, which irreligious we
Let every day decay; and yet we only live
By the great freedoms then those Kings to these did give.

XI:388-98

And in the opening of the twenty-first song Drayton again sang
his lament for the past in the disdain the moderns felt for
antiquity:

That great and ancient Ditch, which us expected long,
Inspired by the Muse, at her arrival song:
O Time, what earthly thing with thee itself can trust,
Then thou in thine one course, art to thyself unjust!
Dost thou contract with death, and to oblivion give
Thy glories, after them, yet shamefully dar'st live?
O Time, hadst thou preserv'd, what labouring man hath
done,
Thou long before this day, mightst to thyself have won
A Deity with the gods, and in thy Temple plac'd,
But sacriligious thou, hast all great works defac'd;
For though the things themselves have suffered by thy
theft,
Yet with their Ruins, thou, to ages mightst have left,
Those Monuments who rear'd, and not have suff'red thus
Posterity so much, t' abuse both thee and us.

XXI:3-16

And in the sixteenth song the River Ver sings her lament for
the past as she wends her way along her banks. Another of the
comments in the poem which continually recalls the golden past
is the constantly recurring reference to the decay of the stately
forests of England as the cities gradually destroy them. Drayton
made this decline synonymous with the degradation of true
poetry and morals under the aegis of James I. In these references
we have a repetition of the satyr's story in the tenth nimphall of
The Muses Elizium, in which he told of the cutting down of the
groves in the oncoming Iron Age and of the approaching destruction of Felicia. These laments for the forests, woods, and
groves occur almost everywhere in *Poly-Olbion.*[3]

Closely allied to this distaste for the evils of modern city life
and to this love for the past is Drayton's appreciation of the

pastoral life. In Song 13 when he described the hermit, so similar to the one in *Elizium*, Drayton brought all of these feelings together:

> To Forests that belongs; but yet this is not all:
> With solitude what sorts, that here's not wondrous rife?
> Whereas the hermit leads a sweet retired life,
> From Villages replete with ragg'd and sweating Clowns,
> And from the loathsome airs of smoky citied Towns.
> Suppose twixt noon and night, the Sun his half-way wrought
> (The shadows to be large, by his descending brought)
> Who with a fervent eye looks through the twyring glades,
> And his dispersed rays commixeth with the shades,
> Exhaling the milch dew, which there had tarried long,
> And on the ranker grass till past the noon-sted hong;
> When as the Hermit comes out of his homely Cell,
> Where from all rude resort he happily doth dwell:
> Who in the strangth of youth, a man of Arms hath seen,
> Retires him from it quite; and with a constant mind
> Man's beastliness so loathes, that flying human kind,
> The black and darksome nights, the bright and gladsome days
> Indifferent are to him, his hope on God that stays.
> Each little Village yields his short and homely fare:
> To gather wind-fall's sticks, his great'st and only care;
> Which ever aged tree still yieldeth to his fire.
> This man, that is alone a King in his desire,
> By no proud ignorant Lord is basely over-aw'd,
> Nor his false praise affects, who grossly being claw'd,
> Stands like an itchy Moyle; nor of a pin he weighs
> What fools, abused Kings, and humourous Ladies raise.
> His free and noble thought, nere envies at the grace
> That often times is given unto a Bawd most base,
> Nor stirs it him to think on the Imposte vile,
> Who seeming what he's not, doth sensually beguile
> The sottish purblind world: but absolutely free,
> His happy time he spends the works of God to see,
> In those so sundry herbs which there in plenty grow:
> Whose sundry strange effects he only seeks to know.
> And in a little Maund, being made of Oziers small,
> Which serveth him to do full many a thing withall,
> He very choicely sorts his Simples got abroad.

XIII:162-99

In other places Drayton emphasized only the joys of the pastoral life itself. Thus in Song 14 he described the pride the shepherds had in their flocks, and then he told of their feast much as he had done in Eclogue IX of 1606:

> But Muse, return to tell, how there the Shepherds King,
> Whose Flock hath chanc't that year the earliest Lamb to
> bring,
> In his gay Bauldrick sits at his low grassy Board,
> With Flawns, Curds, Clowted-cream, and Country dainties
> stor'd:
> And, whilst the Bag-pipe plays, each lusty jocund Swain
> Quaffes Sillibubs in Kans, to all upon the Plain,
> And to their Country-Girls, whose Nosegays they do wear,
> Some Roundelays do sing: the rest, the burthen bear.
>
> XIV:271-78

And in Song 20 there is a nimphall much like those of *The Muses Elizium*. Again Drayton described the sea nymphs, their coronets of flowers, their festive dances, and finally their hymn to Neptune.

In general these pastoral touches are closer to the spirit of Sidney's *Arcadia* than to that of Spenser's *Calendar*. With the exception of the few passages which scorn the decadence of the cities, most of the pastoral effects are those of appreciation of and joy in nature. Drayton seldom involved himself in religious, political, or ethical problems as did Spenser. Rather, Drayton depicted the pastoral atmosphere as a state of thought and action and as a symbol of escape from present realities into the golden past.

Aside from Drayton's appreciation for the idyllic aspect of country life, he continually showed his keen observation of the realities of nature. Thus in Song 13 (ll. 41-86) there is a list of the birds to be seen in Warwickshire; then in Song 25 another list is added of those in Lincolnshire (52-138). In these and other passages Drayton cataloged and described ninety-four different land birds, water- and sea-fowl.[4] And, as in *The Man in the Moon*, Drayton's description of these birds gives the reader a very real sense of first-hand observation. His observations and cataloging of nature and rural events did not stop with this aviary. In Song 13 the aged hermit gathers a long list of herbs and simples for which the purposes are given (199-234). He wrote of garden flowers (15:174-204), and the fruits and culture of orchards (18:174-97); he described agriculture and farming (14:235-78). In a more active mood he described the country sports of hawking (20:311-46), fishing and fowling (25:139-48), hunting (13:93-161), and coursing (23:327-56). In a frolicsome tone he told of the wrestling and hurling (1:238-51), of shepherds at their games (14:21-24), of country dancing (25:261-64), and of singing and music and the instruments used (4:349-68).[5]

The historian and the poet unite in telling of the glories of England's past in *Poly-Olbion*. For example, in Song 22 the River Ouse sings of the great exploits in the civil wars which she has seen. Without any moralizing, the river tells of the battles that occurred near her banks from Hastings in the eleventh century to the return of Henry VII to Bosworth in the fifteenth. Unlike the battles described in his other historical poems, Drayton did not warn of the evils of civil war, but was content in boasting of the glories of English military prowess. Scattered throughout the poem are such descriptions of famous military events which took place in the various sections of England and Wales.

Although in a very real sense this poem is a history of England, the sequence of events is never told merely in a chronological order. Drayton instead made geography his primary basis. Only when the muse approached a particular area did the mountains, rivers, and plains speak up to recount the events of history they themselves had witnessed.

As a poet-geographer Drayton gave to each of the areas, and physical elements within those sections, specific human characteristics. When he described Wrekin, a mountain in Wales, he drew a picture of pride, of aggressiveness softened by love. Two songs later in fourteen Drayton told how the mountain Clent was angered and saddened by the fact that the forest Feckenham loved the River Salwarp rather than himself.

The entire fifteenth song is devoted to a celebration of the nuptials between the rivers Tame and Isis. This song, complete with nuptial hymn, is a lavish imitation of Spenser's marriage of the Medway and the Thames in Book IV, Canto XI of *The Faerie Queene*. In this story the love described is successful as opposed to the many ill-fated love stories told in *Poly-Olbion*. In the twenty-first song, for instance, Drayton told of the mountain

Gogmagog who wooed the River Grant in vain. In this story Drayton exploited the rude country manners and speech of Gogmagog with a great deal of humorous effect:

> . . . When as we met again,
> With one whose constant heart, with cruel love was slain:
> Old Gogmagog, a Hill of long and great renown,
> Which near to Cambridge set, o'rlooks that learned Town.
> Of Balsham's pleasant hill, that by the name was known,
> But with the monstrous times, he rude and barbarous grown,
> A Giant was become; for man he cared not,
> And so the fearful name of Gogmagog had got:
> Who long had bourn good will to most delicious Grant:
> But doubting lest some god his greatness might supplant.
> For as that dainty Flood by Cambridge keeps her course,
> He found the Muses left their old Beotian source,
> Resorting to her banks, and every little space,
> He saw bright Phoebus gaze upon her crystal face,
> And through th' exhaled Fogs, with anger looked red,
> To leave his loved Nymph, when he went down to bed.
> Wherefor this Hill with love, being foully overgone:
> And one day as he found the lovely Nymph alone,
> Thus wooes her: Sweeting mine, if thou mine own wilt be,
> C'have many a pretty gaud, I keep in store for thee.
> A nest of broad-fac'd Owls, and goodly Urchins too;
> Nay Nymph take heed of me, when I begin to woo:
> And better yet then this, a Bulchin twa years old,
> A curld-pate Calf it is, and oft could have been sold:
> And yet besides all this, c'have goodly Bear-whelps twa,
> Full dainty for my Joy, when she dispos'd to play,
> And twentie Sows of Lead, to make our wedding Ring;
> Besides a Sturbridge Fayre, chill buy thee many a thing:
> Chill zmouch thee every morne, before the Sun can rise,
> And look my manly face, in thy sweet glaring eyes.
>   Thus said, he smug'd his Beard, and stroked up his hair,
> As one that for her love he thought had offered fair:
> Which to the Muses, Grant did presently report,
> Wherewith they many a year shall make them wondrous sport.

XXI:43-76

Structurally, the poem consists of thirty songs. Each of these is prefaced with a verse argument of six to twenty lines in tetrameter couplets. Then the song itself is written in iambic hexameter couplets ranging from 290 to 1638 lines, accompanied by Drayton's customary marginal gloss. Prefacing each of the songs is a map taken from Saxton's *Atlas* of 1579. And following each of the first eighteen songs are a total of 169 pages of learned notes by the antiquarian John Selden. In all the total length of the poem, excluding prose notes, is 14,990 lines consisting of 374 lines of argument and 14,616 lines of the actual songs.

Another problem frequently discussed in relation to Drayton's *Poly-Olbion* is whether or not it can be considered as an epic poem. Lewis Ball doubtfully maintains that it can, on the basis of Classical and Renaissance theory and practice.[6] In this major poem Drayton united topography with all of the required elements of the epic. First of all he chose the hexameter which had been the meter of such great epics as *The Iliad, The Odyssey,* and *The Aeneid,* and which had been recommended by Ronsard as the proper meter for an epic poem. It also fulfilled the requirement of length. No one would seriously deny that the almost fifteen thousand lines constituted sufficient length for an epic. Drayton, in addition, followed the traditional divisions of the Canto or Songs.

The motif of patriotism is as much present in *Poly-Olbion* as in any of the Classical epics. Certainly Drayton's basic purpose was to glorify England and her history. But unlike the great epics of the past Drayton's poem has no central character who might embody the spirit of England. In fact, properly speaking, there are no characters as such in this poem.

The appeal to the Muses, and invocations are not forgotten in this work; and, of course, the epic requirement for an heroic catalog is amply fulfilled. In addition to the listing of birds previously mentioned, the poem contains catalogs of English warriors in Song 17, British kings in 8, the Blazons of the Shires in 23, English naval explorers in 9, and English Saints in 24.

Drayton also used similes and continually exploited the uses of gods, goddesses, and their attendant spirits. Finally, Drayton's contemporaries considered that *Poly-Olbion* was an epic. In his conversations with Jonson, Drummond of Hawthornden wrote that it was the only epic of which England could be proud.[7] And for this work William Browne and George Wither commended Drayton as the English Vergil or Homer.[8]

However, although this work contains all the machinery of the epic, it is missing two essentials. The poem does not have an epic hero, nor does it tell a specific story. Rather than call it an epic, we might say that *Poly-Olbion* is a unique product of the Elizabethan literary patriot in that it fuses the topographical, historical, and legendary materials of England and Wales on a colossal scale.

Although this work was unique, many of the poets who knew Drayton used this work to assist them in composing their own poems which contained topographical elements. None of these other works ever attempted or achieved the magnitude of Drayton's work. From 1617 on John Taylor, the water poet, spent thirty-five years traveling about England and writing about the landscape. In the foreword to his *Taylor on Thame Isis* in which he wrote of the hindrances on the journey between Oxford and London, he gave credit to Drayton:

> Of learned Camden, Speed, and Holinshead
> And Drayton's painful Poly-Olbion,
> Whose fame shall live, despite oblivion.
> These are the guides I follow with pretence
> T'abbreviate and extract their Quint-essence.[9]

The Drayton poem also influenced William Slatyer's *History of Great Britanniae* or *Palae-Albion* in 1621. The anonymous and undated "The origins and progress of the river Tawmer" is another which drew heavily upon *Poly-Olbion*. In both of these are nymphs, amours of river and plain, and a regard for the English past.[10]

Even after Drayton's death poets continued to draw upon his great work whenever they wrote poetry of a topographical nature. Some of those who admitted their indebtedness to the Renaissance poet were Sir John Denham in *Cooper's Hill* in 1642, James Howell's *Prosopopeia to Chesire* in 1664, William King's *Thame and Isis* in 1710, other river descriptions by Nicholas Rowe and George Jeffrey in 1719-21. Alexander Pope drew upon the *Poly-Olbion* in his *Windsor Forest* in 1713. And finally the Reverend Richard Warner ended *Hengistburg Head* with Drayton's marriage of the Avon and the Stour.

Poly-Olbion is not the kind of poem which can be read from beginning to end with no respite. Rather it is a poem best enjoyed by reading carefully chosen selections. For instance, if one is interested in the lake country, then a reading of Song 30 becomes a delight; or perhaps an interest in Shakespeare's home will quicken an interest in Song 13 which relates the glories of Warwickshire.

Since each song is preceded by a map and an argument, perusal of these will easily enable the reader to choose that song which describes the region about which he wishes to read. John Buxton and J. William Hebel also suggest that *Poly-Olbion* is an ideal companion to the English traveler who desires to enjoy fully the wealth of the English and Welsh countryside.

CHAPTER 5

Religious Poems, Occasional Poems, Satires, Odes, and Elegies

I *Religious Poems*

D RAYTON'S excursions into the realm of religious poetry
were not frequent. He published *The Harmonie of the
Church* in 1591; *Moyses in a Map of His Miracles* in 1604, *Noahs
Floud* in 1630, and *David and Goliah* [*sic*] in the same year.

The Harmonie of the Church was a group of close paraphrases
of biblical songs, hymns, and prayers which Drayton set to English meter to be "read or sung." This work was in the general
Renaissance tradition of biblical paraphrase. Drayton's basic
contribution to the genre was in his choice of material. He did
not select the psalms of David for his translations as had many
of his contemporaries, but rather he went farther afield and
achieved an originality of choice in using the lesser known
prayers of prophets and other holy men and women.

In this work Drayton used the old metrical patterns of the
Native school of Elizabethan poetry. Of the twenty poems which
make up this work, Drayton used the fourteener which had previously been used in *The Book of Common Prayer* in 1562 for
the metrical version of the psalms and was also popular in the
many anthologies of the period. The poulter's measure, consisting of alternate heptameter and hexameter lines, was used in
"The Song of Judith" and in the eight sections of "The Song of
Salomon." In "Moses," "Tobias," and "Mardocheus" Drayton used
the sixain. He also composed some of the poems in either tetrameter or pentameter quatrains.

Glenn Percival Haskell has identified the Geneva Bible as the
primary source for Drayton's paraphrase;[1] whereas Hebel and
Tillotson also suggested the Bishops' Bible as another source.[2]
The metrical paraphrases are, as Drayton himself stated in his
preface, "so exactly translated as the prose would permit, or

sense would any way suffer me." About the only liberties which Drayton took with the biblical text was to add adjectives which filled out the meter. In his choice of adjectives, he too frequently used those which gave his line an alliterative effect. The excessive regularity of his lines makes reading these poems very monotonous, but since he intended them to be put to music and sung, this regularity can perhaps be forgiven. Nowhere in Drayton's poetry is his difficulty with syntax more evident than in these poems, his first offerings to his public. He continually wrenched the word order and the sense in his attempts to achieve his rhyme.

"The Praier of Salomon" from the ninth chapter of the Book of Wisdom illustrates Drayton's syntactic difficulties and the general style of the many mediocre passages:

> For I thy servant am, and of thy handmaid borne,
> A silly soul, whose life alas, is short and all forlorn.
> And do not understand at all, what ought to be my guide,
> I mean thy statutes and thy laws, least that I slip aside.
> For though a man in worldly things, for wisdom be esteem'd,
> Yet if thy wisdom want in him, his, is but folly deem'd.
>
> ll. 9-14

Three of the paraphrases stand out as much better than the remainder, "The Song of the Israelites," "The most excellent Song of Salomon," and "A Song of Jhesus the son of Sirach." The latter shows Drayton's earliest work in its best light:

> I have been succoured by thee,
> And thou hast still preserved me:
> And from destruction kept me long,
> And from report of slanderous tongue.
>
> From lips stil exercis'd with lies,
> And from my cruel enemies,
> Thou me in mercy dost deliver,
> Thy blessed name be prais'd for ever.
>
> ll. 5-12

He reissued these poems with a very few syntactic changes in 1610, and then finally consigned them to a deserved oblivion. The most noteworthy thing about this collection of religious poems was that soon after its first publication it was, for some unknown reason, seized by public order and destroyed with forty copies being preserved at Lambeth. *The Harmonie of the Church* thus became a footnote to the history of Elizabethan religious prejudice.

In 1604 Drayton published his second religious work, *Moyses in a Map of His Miracles.* Like his other two biblical stories of 1630, this poem fitted into a stream of Renaissance literature which reacted against the pagan elements derived from the imitations of the classics. In these works, Drayton generally followed the lead of DuBartas' *Judith* and *La Semaine,* and he found himself in the company of Francis Quarles' stories of Jonah, Job, Samson, and Esther written in the 1620's.

Unlike *The Harmonie of the Church* Drayton's later religious works were very free adaptations of the original and not translations. Rather they were amplifications and variations based upon the biblical stories. In these works Drayton was not concerned with an exposition of Christian theology as was found in Giles Fletcher's *Christ's Victory and Triumph,* nor was he didactic like Phineas Fletcher in *The Purple Island.* Drayton did not attempt to teach by either allegory or symbol. His primary purpose was to tell one of the stories which formed the Judaic foundation of Christianity. There was no sectarianism as in the poetry of George Herbert, nor religious fervor as in the poems of Robert Southwell or John Donne. Drayton merely elaborated on a sacred subject.

Written in a basic iambic pentameter with irregular verse stanzas rhymed *ababcdcdef etc., Moyses in a Map of His Miracles* is 2270 lines long including thirty lines of tetrameter argument and is divided into three books. This work is full of heterogeneous elements. In the first book we are told the story of the birth and youth of Moses in the fashion of a sentimental late Medieval romance. The narrative moves quickly in the early pages with occasional pauses for descriptive passages. One of the best of these tells of the joy of the babe's mother on receiving her own child back in her arms:

> This while all mute, the poore astonish'd Mother,
> With admiration as transpierced stood,
> One bursting joy doth so confound another,
> Passion so powerful in her ravish'd blood,

Whisp'ring some soft words which delivered were,
As rather seem'd her silence to impart,
And being inforc'd from bashfulness and fear,
Came as true tokens of a graceful heart.
Thus she departs her husband to content,
With this dear present back to him she brought,
Making the time short, telling each event,
In all shapes joy presented to her thought.

I:373-85

In the section where Moses is in exile at Midian, the poet drew a picture of Arcadian bliss with fair shepherdesses in a pastoral setting, and gave a long description of the beauties of the young Moses.

In the second book Moses brings the message of Jehovah to the Pharaoh's court, and the prophet calls down the ten plagues when the message is ignored. After the second plague the poet halts and calls upon his Muse to reflect upon the difficulty involved in maintaining decorum in reciting the horrors of the plagues:

But stay my Muse in height of all this speed,
Somewhat plucks back to quench this sacred heat,
And many perils doth to us areed
In that whereof we seriously entreat.
Lest too concise injuriously we wrong
Things that such state and fearfulness impart,
Or led by zeal irregularly long,
Infringe the curious liberties of Art,
We that calumnious Critic may eschew,
That blasteth all things with his pois'ned breath,
Detracting what laboriously we do,
Only with that which he but idly saith.
O be our guide whose glories now we preach,
That above Books must steer us in our Fate,
For never Ethnic to this day did teach,
(In this) whose method we might imitate.

II:157-72

The descriptions of the plagues themselves were from biblical sources, and probably some of the details came from Drayton's own observations of the London plague in 1603. Especially graphic is the passage which recounts some of the effects of the sixth plague, the murrain which affected both beasts and men. In the third book Drayton recounted the flight from Egypt and the wandering in the desert until the death of Moses.

Drayton's touch was deft in recounting his story, and at times the physical details drew a dramatic picture in the minds of the readers. However, this is an interesting but not really good poem, as it seems to lack a unifying motivation which would give it life.

In 1630, together with the little revised *Moyses*, Drayton published two other religious poems, *Noahs Floud* and *David and Goliah* [sic]. In the first, we have a retelling of the story of the flood. Drayton used material from DuBartas' description of the animals at creation, from the lore of the bestiaries, and from his own observations. In Drayton's menagerie all of the animals are well drawn and given specific characteristics:

> The skipping Squerrill of the Forest free,
> That leapt so nimbly betwixt tree and tree,
> It self into the Ark then nimbly cast,
> As 'twere a Ship-boy come to clime the Mast.
> The Porcupine into the Ark doth make,
> Nor his sharp quills though angry once doth shake;
> The sharp-fang'd Beaver, whose wide gaping Jaw
> Cutteth down Plants as were with a Saw,
> Whose body poised, weigheth such a mass,
> As though his Bowels were of Lead or Brass,
> His cruel Chaps though breathless he doth close,
> As with the rest into the Ark he goes.
> Th' uneven-leg'd Badger (whose eye-pleasing skin,
> The Case to many a curious thing hath bin,
> Since that great flood) his fortresses forsakes
> Wrought in the earth, and though but halting, makes
> Up to the Ark; the Otter then that keeps
> In the wild Rivers, in their Banks and Sleeps,
> And feeds on Fish, which under water still,
> He with his keld feet, and keen teeth doth kill;
> The other two into the Ark doth follow,
> Though his ill shape doth cause him but to wallow;
> The Tortoise and the Hedgehog both so slow,
> As in their motions scarce discern'd to go,
> Good footmen grown, contrary to their kind,
> Lest from the rest they should be left behind;
>
> ll. 323-48

Aside from the catalog of the animals, the best part of the 1052-line poem is the actual description of the flood itself when the heavens opened and the rains poured down. In 130 lines (ll. 633-762) Drayton drew a highly realistic picture of what the effects of the great tempest were. In addition to the story the poet tells, there is also the mark of the scholar. Drayton offered an explanation of the flood and the size of the ark (ll. 513ff.) to the non-believer. Also in his frequent marginal notes, he cited authorities for his statements and at times offered a moralizing gloss on the text of his poem.

The last religious poem, *David and Goliah,* is certainly Drayton's best in this genre. The poet found his basic source in the first book of Samuel and made the story into a lively combination of a pastoral and martial tale. In this work are many fine descriptive passages such as this which pictured David guarding his flocks:

> Whether in Cotes he had his flock in hold,
> Or for the Fallowes kept them in the fold,
> He was not idle, though not taking pains,
> Celestial Lyricks singing to the Swains,
> And often sitting in the silent shade,
> When his fair flock to rest themselves were laid,
> On his Lyre tuned such harmonious Lays,
> That the Birds pearcht upon the tender sprays,
> Mad at his music, strain themselves so much
> To imitate th' unimitable touch,
> Breaking their hearts, that they have dropt to ground,
> And died for grief in malicing the sound.
> Sometimes a Stag he with his Sling would slay,
> Or with his Sheephook kill a Boar at bay,
> Or run a Roe so long (he was so fleet)
> Till it lay trembling, breathless, at his feet,
> Sometimes again, he practised a fight,
> That from the Desert, should a Dragon light
> Upon his Sheep, the Serpent to assail,
> How by cleer skill through courage to prevail.
> Then with a small stone thrown out of his Sling
> To hit a swallow on her height of wing,
>
> ll. 79-100

The fight between David and the giant is also very well done. Drayton first emphasized the incongruity of the struggle by stressing the grace and slightness of the shepherd as opposed to the ferocity and immense bulk of Goliath. Finally David steps forward to fight the giant:

> In meantime David looking in his face
> Between his temples, saw how large a space
> He was to hit, steps back a yard or two,
> The Giant wondring what the Youth would do,
> Whose nimble hand, out of his Scrip doth bring
> A pebble stone, and puts it in his Sling,
> At which the Giant openly doth jeer,
> And as in scorn, stands leaning on his Spear,
> Which gives young David much content to see,
> And to himself thus secretly saith he,
> Stand but one minute still, stand but so fast,
> And have at all Philistia at a cast.
> When with such slight the shot away he sent,
> That from his Sling as't had been Lightning went;
> And him so full upon the forehead smit,
> Which gave a crack, when his thick scalp it hit,
> As t'had been thrown against some Rock or Post,
> That the shrill clap was heard through either host.
> Staggering a while upon his Spear he leant,
> Till on a sudden, he began to faint;
> When down he came, like an old o're growne Oak,
> His huge Root hewn up by the Labourers stroke,
> That with his very weight, he shook the ground,
> His brazen armour gave a jarring sound
> Like a crackt Bell, or vessel chanc't to fall
> From some high place, which did like death apall
> The proud Philistians, (hopeless that remain)
> To see their Champion great Goliah slain:
> When such a shout the host of Israel gave,
> As cleft the clouds, and like to men that rave,
> (O'rcome with comfort) cry, the Boy, the Boy,
> O the brave David, Israels only joy:
> Gods chosen Champion, O most wondrous thing,
> The great Goliah slain with a poor Sling:

ll. 757-90

Of all the religious poems this story of *David and Goliah* is Drayton's most original and best written. In this work he discarded all extraneous information and learned comment and kept solely to his tale. His use of the pentameter couplet in this poem was smooth and effective. He varied the caesura, and gave the line further flexibility with a judicious use of end stops and enjambment. Even today these lines retain their attraction for the reader. The careful use of the meter together with a fluid combination of description and action make *David and Goliah* well worth reading.

II *Occasional Poems*

Drayton did not write many occasional poems. With the exception of seventeen short poems written as commendatory verses for other poets and translators, there are only two which he wrote for special occasions.

To The Majestie of King James was written to celebrate the accession of James the First to the throne of England in 1603. It is a conventional piece which could have been written by any poet of the period who was seeking the favor of the new King. However, it does have a special place in that it is the only poem in praise of the new King which omitted the customary praise of the late Queen (and this before she was even buried!). In 176 lines of pentameter couplets, Drayton traced the ancestry of the new King, carefully ignoring his mother's untimely death. He praised James as the symbol of the union of the white rose of York with the red rose of Lancaster. Then he urged the King to cleanse the court of undesirable elements:

> The very earthl'est & degenerat'st spirit,
> That is most void of virtue, and of merit,
> With the auster'st, and impudentest face,
> Will thrust himself the formost to thy grace;
> Those silken, laced, and perfumed hinds,
> That have rich bodies, but poor wretched minds,
> But from thy Court (O Worthy) banish quite
> The fool, that Pandar, and the Parasite,
> And call thyself most happy (then be bold)
> When worthy places, worthi'st men do hold,
> The servile clown for shame shall hide his head,
> His ignorance, and baseness frustrated,
> Set lovely virtue ever in thy view,
> And love them most, that most do her pursue,
> So shalt thou add renown unto thy state,
> A King most great, most wise, most fortunate.

ll. 161-76

Unfortunately for Drayton his untimely omission of praise for Elizabeth caused a chorus of other poets to mock his lack of taste and tact. Also his hope of seeing King James improve the caliber of the court was quickly dashed.

His second occasional poem, *A Paean Triumphall* was written on behalf of the goldsmiths of London for the first royal entry of the King into London in 1603-4. The King himself is little mentioned in the poem; the emphasis is on the goldsmiths' guild and a description of a London in celebration:

> Whil'st Temples stand even trembling as afeard,
> To see proud Pageants on their arches reard
> Above their Turrets, whilst the concourse meet,
> Like boisterous tides in every public street.
> Windows of eyes, the houses scorn'd their glass,
> On every side their Majesties should pass:
> Rooms with rich beauties furnished about,
> Arras but serves to hang the walls without.
> Who lov'd in works of ancient times to prie,
> Hangings complete with curious Imagrie,
> Glutting his eyes here lively might behold,
> Faces whose numbers figures never told,
> Walling the houses, in whose several eyes
> Joy shewes it self in more varieties,
> Then be their minds, the objects that they see,
> Which are as various as their features be.
> The high-rear'd spires shake with the peoples cry,
> Bending their tops seem wondring to espy
> Streets pav'd with heads, for such the numbers be,
> The loftiest Tower no ground at all can see.
> Banners, Flags, Streamers, in such numbers borne,
> And stood so thick that one might soon have sworn,
> Nature of late some novelty had brought,
> Groves leav'd with silk in curious manner wrought,
> Bearing such fruit th' Atlantides did keep,
> By that fierce Dragon that did never sleep.

> ll. 23-48

In addition to these two occasional poems Drayton wrote seventeen poems as commendatory verse for other authors. In most of these verses Drayton praised the ability of the author and suggested to the reader why the volume was worth reading. In these brief efforts Drayton used many metrical forms: sonnets, quatrains, and couplets. In one case, in the verse for Thomas Morley's *First Booke of Ballets to Five Voyces*, Drayton used an unusual nine-line verse. The rhymes, *abbaccbdd*, are all feminine, and lines 1, 2, 3, 5, and 7 are trimeter with lines 4, 6, 8, and 9 in pentameter. In the verse for Sir John Davies, who was a frequent correspondent with Drayton, the poet puns as he comments on the pernicious practice of exchanging commendatory verses:

> Such men as hold intelligence with Letters
> And in that nice and Narrow way of Verse,
> As oft they lend, so oft they must be Debtors,
> If with the Muses they will have commerce:
> Seldom at Stawles me, this way men rehearse,
> To mine Inferiours, nor unto my Betters:
> He stales his lines that so doth them disperse;
> I am so free, I love not Golden-fetters:
> And many Lines fore Writers, be but Setters
> To them which Cheat with Papers; which doth pierse,
> Our Credits: when we shew our selves Abetters:
> To those that wrong our knowledge: we rehearse
> > Often (my good John; and I love) thy Letters;
> > Which lend me Credit, as I lend my Verse.

In general Drayton's commendatory verses are neither particularly interesting nor outstanding poems. However, this lack of exceptional quality seems to be the rule for the vast majority of commendatory verses written by the Renaissance poets.

One other lyric which cannot be classified in any particular category, and which was never published by Drayton, was written by him the night before he died. In seven pentameter tercets, the poet recalls the love he bore Idea. The conceit in the poem fits easily into the metaphysical strain:

> So well I love thee, as without thee I
> Love nothing, if I might choose, I'd rather die
> Than be one day debard thy company
>
> Since Beasts, and plants do grow, and live and move
> Beasts are those men, that such a life approve
> He only Lives, that Deadly is in Love
>
> The Corn that in the ground is sown first dies
> And of one seed do many Ears arise
> Love this world's Corn, by dying Multiplies

The seeds of Love first by thy eyes were thrown
Into a grownd untild, a heart unknown
To bear such fruit, till by thy hands t'was sown

Look as your Looking glass by Chance may fall
Divide and break in many pieces small
And yet shews forth, the self same face in all

Proportions, Features Grace just the same
And in the smalest piece as well the name
Of Fairest one deserves, as in the richest frame

So all my Thoughts are pieces but of you
Which put together makes a Glass so true
As I therin no others face but yours can View.

III *Satires*

Drayton wrote two poems which fit primarily into the satiric mode: *The Owle*, published in 1604, and *The Moon-calfe* from the 1627 edition of his poems. Aside from these two, there are several scattered passages of satire in his other works; as instanced by the poet in *The Man in the Moon* peering down upon the vices of earth. Also in *The Shepheards Sirena* and *Poly-Olbion* Drayton satirized poets who debased their talents and poets who refused to publish their work. Again in the fourth and tenth nimphalls of *The Muses Elizium* he attacked the excesses of the court.

In *The Owle* Drayton used the Medieval springtime vision and the bird fable as the framework to carry his satire. In his address to the reader the poet suggested that *The Owle* was in the same genre as the Greek classic *Batrachomachia* and the Roman *Culex*. The modern reader is also reminded of such works as Chaucer's *The Parlement of Foules*, Sir Richard Holland's *The Buke of The Howlat*, and Spenser's *Mother Hubbard's Tale*. John Skelton had also used a bird to mouth his satirical comments in his *Speke Parrot*, as had Robert Henryson in *The Preaching of the Swallow*.

The poem opens on a spring day in the woods, where the poet has a vision of the gathering of the birds whom he can understand. For the first 150 lines the poem without any hint of satire describes the birds in their sylvan setting; then the next hundred lines contain glimpses of it. Finally as the owl makes his complaint to the eagle, the satire becomes manifest. First the evils at court are aired, then those of the countryside, and finally those of the city. The poem ends with the incident of the fall of the oak and the morals drawn by the owl and the eagle. Even when the satire is most evident, the birds retain their own identities. In fact, this ability to discover those natural habits of the birds, illustrating the human evils which the poet depicts is one of the strongest points of Drayton's work.

In the satirical passages, the topical references to specific individuals are highly elusive, but the poet's view of general abuses is easily seen. Thus his many subjects, the luxury of the rich at court, the cruelty of the monopolists of the city, oppression by the landlords in the country, flattery, religious persecution, and sexual license are all easily discoverable by the reader.

Specific individual identification of the major birds in the poem has been a problem which has intrigued many scholars. Although Hebel and Tillotson have pointed out that insufficient clues are given in the poem for complete and absolute identification, students of the period have continued their search for answers. Ray L. Heffner for example suggested that the cock was Sir Philip Sidney:[3]

> But in the Cock which death untimely wrackt,
> In him was both the Elegance and Act,
> O! when that Bird was ravish'd from our sight,
> (Intombing him) the World intomb'd Delight.
> Let never mournful Accent pass my Pen,
> That leaves his Fame un-registered to Men.
>
> ll. 1281-86

However, Harrison in his study of Drayton's birds concluded that several of the birds represented types rather than specific individuals. Thus the kestrel is a rack-renting landlord; the cormorant, a monopolist; the sparrow, a lecherous courtier.[4]

This satire was popular in its day, and may have been a partial influence in works as T. M.'s *Father Hubbards Tales* in 1604-09, Richard Niccol's *The Beggar's Ape* in 1607, *The Cuckow* also of 1607, Thomas Scot's *Philomythie* in 1610-16, and William Goddard's *Owles Arraygnment* of 1616.[5]

If the modern reader is aware of the general economic and social conditions which existed in the English court and country in 1603, he can still read this satire with a great deal of enjoyment. For Drayton had his material well under control, and combined his satire well with his knowledge of aviary lore. The poem only becomes dull when the reader attempts to identify each bird. It is not the specific individual references which give the poem its savor, but rather those references which apply to the continuing vices of mankind. Indeed we always have the lecherous, the greedy, the ambitious; and the birds Drayton described are still symbolic of the same kind of behavior.

In 1627 Drayton published *The Moon-calfe.* This satire is actually divided into two parts. The first section is a Swiftian satire on the birth of the Moon-calfe, and the second is a group of four *exempla.* The poem opens with the description of the world in labor. She is giving birth to a monster, the Moon-calfe, sired by the devil. The poet attendant at this birth looks to the future and foresees the vices and absurdities in which the Moon-calfe will be involved. First he describes the male Moon-calfe's follies in the extravagance, luxury, and license of the court. Then he depicts the female of the species with her ludicrous fashions and complete lack of morals. He thus describes the female Moon-calfe at her toilet:

> But her own natural beauty she disdains,
> With Oils and Broths most venomous and base,
> She plasters over her well-favoured face;
> And those sweet veins by nature rightly plac'd,
> Wherewith she seem'd that white skin to have lac'd,
> She soon doth alter; and with fading blew,
> Blanching her bosom, she makes others new;
> Blotting the curious workmanship of nature;
> That e're she be arriv'd at her full stature,
> E're she be drest, she seemeth aged grown,
> And to have nothing on her of her own:
> Her black, browne, auburn or her yellow hair,
> Naturally lovely, she doth scorn to wear;
> It must be white to make it fresh to show,
> And with compounded meal she makes it so:
> With fumes and powdrings raising such a smoke,
> That a whole Region able were to choke:
> Whose stench might fright a Dragon from his den,
> The Sun yet ne're exhal'd from any Fen;
> Such pestilencious vapours as arise,
> From their French Powdrings, and their Mercuries.
>
> ll. 462-82

Then after he tells of the ridiculous fashions in clothes, he lampoons her morals:

> The very sight of her when she doth roar,
> Is able to strike dumb the boldest Whore
> That ever traded: she'll not stick to tell,
> All in her life that ever her befell;
> How she hath lain, with all degrees, and ages,
> Her Plow-Boys, Scullians, Lackies, and some Pages,
> And swear when we have said all that we can,
> That there is nothing worth a pin in man,
> And that there's nothing doth so please her mind,
> As to see Mares, and Horses, do their kind;
> And when she's Tipsy, how so e're t'offend,
> Then all her speech to Bawdry doth intend:
> In Womens secrets, and she'll name ye all
> Read to the Midwives at the Surgeons Hall.
>
> ll. 555-68

The second part of the poem (ll. 575-1390) is closely related to the Medieval exemplum. The four old women who acted as midwives at the birth of the Moon-calfe sit around the fire, and each tells a tale with a moral attached. Mother Redcap first relates how a sane man went to a village where everyone acted in an insane manner. When he remonstrated with the villagers on the madness of their actions, they accused him of being mad. The moral was drawn that whoever departs from the norm, whether it be good or bad, is considered as in the wrong.

Mother Bumby then tells of a witch and her accomplice, an ape, who practiced all kinds of villainies with great success. Finally a wise astronomer created two spirit images of the witch and the ape. When the spirits confronted their adversaries, the spirit witch versus the ape and the spirit ape versus the witch, the spirits frightened the villains so that they fled the land. The moral was that divine justice finally conquers those who through ambition and greed have sold themselves to the devil.

Mother Owle tells of a wicked man who obtained the power of changing himself into a werewolf. He preyed upon the countryside, destroying man, woman, and beast. Finally, a good man who had been turned into an ass by a witch discovered the villain's secret and brought about his downfall. The moral was drawn that just souls, who are frequently disdained by the world, are often God's instruments in revealing wickedness.

The last exemplum is told by Gammer Gurton. A group of starving cattle, asses, and mules live in a wasteland. Finally, they break into a lush meadow where they feast until they are driven out by the farmer and impounded. In this way the newly rich misuse their ill-gotten gains until they finally end up in prison.

The first half of this satire on the foibles and fashions is dull and conventional after the style of Joseph Hall and John Marston. However, the second half with its morality tales has a greater good humor and can be read with some ease. In all this satire offers no new contribution to the genre in either style or content.

IV *Odes*

In the twenty lyrics which Drayton published under the heading of Odes, he once again pioneered in a genre relatively new to English literature. It is true that in the 1580's John Southern had attempted Pindaric odes which Drayton admired but did not emulate. Drayton's contribution was rather the changing of the Horatian ode into an English genre. That he was well aware of what he did is manifest in the preface to the 1606 edition of his odes. Drayton carefully defined the Pindaric, the Anacreontic, and the Horatian odes, and pointed his determination to write mainly the Horatian.

Drayton used Horace primarily for the determination of the basic model, but he also used other poets to assist him. Thus he drew upon Ronsard and the members of the Pleiade for many of his metrical patterns and for some of his themes. Thus "Sing wee the Rose," "To Cupid," and "An Amouret Anacreontick" draw upon the French love lyrics. From Skelton, Drayton borrowed his frequent use of the short line; for this he pays his tribute in entitling one of the odes, "A Skeltoniad." In addition to these odes, Drayton used the odes for expressions of friendship, battle, good cheer, valor, and poetic analysis.

There is no doubt that he did borrow heavily from the French lyric forms, but in most cases the content and expression in his odes were original with him. Sir Sidney Lee overstated his position from one or two minor instances of borrowing, and Samuel R. Shafer merely reflects Lee's position.[6] Of the other revisions for this later edition, Drayton's purpose in reworking the odes was to smooth out the lines and simplify the syntax.

Of the two poems which were dropped in the revised edition, "Sing we the Rose" gives the better picture of Drayton's early work in this genre. Written in nine six-line strophes using monometer and feminine rhymes, the poem highlights his difficulties with his syntax. The first two stanzas amply illustrate both the charm of the lyric as well as its weaker points:

> Sing we the Rose
> Than which no flower there grows
> Is sweeter:
> And aptly her compare
> With what in that is rare
> A parallel none meeter.
>
> Or made poses,
> Of this that incloses
> Such blisses,
> That naturally flusheth
> As she blusheth
> When she is rob'd of kisses.
>
> ll. 1-12

"The Heart" is one of the poet's most successful odes and is frequently anthologized. In it Drayton dealt with a metaphysical fancy closely paralleling that of certain Donne lyrics. The conceit is of two broken hearts which have been mended into one. Thus one of the lovers must be heartless until the other relieves him:

> Half this is of your Heart,
> Mine in the other part,
> Joyn'd by our equal Art.
>
> Were it cemented, or sown,
> By Shreds or Pieces known,
> We each might find our own.
>
> But 'tis dissolv'd, and fix'd,
> And with such cunning mix'd,
> No diff'rence that betwixt.
>
> But how shall we agree,
> By whom it kept shall be,
> Whether by you, or me?

> It cannot two Breasts fill,
> One must be heartless still,
> Until the other will.
>
> It came to me today,
> When I will'd it to say,
> With whether it would stay?
>   ll. 7-24

"The Cryer" has a similar metaphysical conceit in which the poet hires a crier to find his lost heart. The unusual treatment in the lyric makes the heart a separate entity which has been wounded by love and has run away with the object of its love. "To His Rivall" is a delightful ode which scoffs at the inconstancy of women, in a definite Cavalier tone. The last four of the nine strophes give the full flavor of the poem:

> I had the vow
> That thou hast now,
> And Glances to discover
> Her Love to me,
> And she to thee
> Reads but old Lessons over.
>
> She hath no Smile
> That can beguile,
> But as my Thought I know it;
> Yea, to a Hair,
> Both when and where,
> And how she will bestow it.
>
> What now is thine,
> Was only mine,
> And first to me was given;
> Thou laugh'st at me,
> I laugh at thee,
> And thus we two are even.
>
> But I'll not mourn,
> But stay my Turn,
> The Wind may come about, Sir,
> And once again
> May bring me in,
> And help to bear you out, Sir.
>   ll. 31-54

The ode, "To the Virginian Voyage," is one of the best poems in the entire Drayton canon. In this lyric of 1606 he discarded the ornate trappings of the Petrarchan school which had dominated his early lyrics. True, there still remained some of the syntactic difficulties he never managed to eradicate completely; but compared with that of the early sonnets and his long historical works, the language is relatively simple. He eschewed the classical and mythological allusions which had commonly appeared in his work. In the entire seventy-two lines of this ode there are only two such references: "when Aeolus scowls" and "Apollo's sacred tree." The blatant and artificial metaphors were replaced with more subtle and effective figures:

> And the ambitious Vine
> Crowns with his purple Mass,
>   The Cedar reaching high
>   To kiss the Sky,
> The Cypress, Pine
> And useful Sassafras.
>
> . . . . . .
>
> When as the Lushious smell
> Of that delicious Land,
>   Above the Seas that flows,
>   The clear Wind throws,
> Your Hearts to swell
> Approaching the dear Strand.
>
> ll. 31-36, 43-48

The sensory image in the latter strophe given by *lushious* and *delicious* as connected to *land* when carried by the *wind* over the *seas* is real and refreshing. The poet kept his eye and mind on the subject; he did not try to inflate the subject with extravagant diction. Since the poet was applying a common concept to a particular situation, the poem achieved a feeling of universality. In this poem Drayton wedded the best qualities of both the Native and the Petrarchan schools. In the year when the ode was first published three ships had sailed under the Virginian patent; and this event, colored by Drayton's reading of Hakluyt, led to the writing of this poem. In this work Drayton transcends the subject of the immediate voyage and pays honor to all voyagers who travel unknown seas in search of honor.

Even more popular than the latter ode is Drayton's "To the Cambro-Britons, and their Harpe, his Ballad of Agincourt," more commonly known as "The Ballad of Agincourt." Drayton published this poem with his odes, in that it was a poem in praise of valor. Yet, since the metrical form was similar to some fifteenth-century ballads and since it also filled the ballad requirement of being a portion of a known story, he called it a ballad. The subject matter is well known; Drayton's long historical poem, *The Battaile of Agincourt*, renders all of the details. In the 120 lines of this poem Drayton condensed all of the martial spirit and glory which England won on that St. Crispin's day.

Drayton achieved a verse form eminently suitable for the martial beat of the poem. The shortness of the trimeter and dimeter lines with the trisyllabic feet in the dimeter lines together with the frequency of the triple recurring rhyme increases the feeling of urgency in the poem's action. Lines 89-120 with its catalog of English heroes, form the high point of the poem. The deliberately archaic flavor of the poem and the ballad style increase the emotional level of the poem as a recounting of one of England's most glorious moments. As in "To the Virginian Voyage" Drayton here managed a perfect balance between the values of the subject and the evoked emotion. In this case the subject is heroic, and so are the emotions charging through the lines.

In these odes Drayton achieved several lyrics of exceptionally high quality which add to his stature as a lyric poet. And his poetic range in these odes reached into treatment of both the Cavalier and the Metaphysical poets.

V *Elegies*

In the 1627 edition of Drayton's poems were twelve elegies, two of which, "Upon the Death of the Lady Penelope Clifton" and "Upon . . . the Three Sonnes of the Lord Sheffield," had been published earlier in the 1618 and 1620 edition of an anthology, *Certain Elegies, done by sundrie Excellent Wits.*[7] Including the two aforementioned, five elegies were written on the occasion of someone's death. The other seven were friendly epistles written in the Horatian manner.

Funeral elegies customarily followed a set pattern. After an opening invocation or apostrophe, the deceased's life was praised;

nobility of birth, education in youth, prowess in young manhood, service to mankind, and a virtuous death were all included in the panegyric. Drayton's funeral elegies did not conform at all to this pattern; in fact, in his elegies there was no set pattern, except that all seem to have been written with sincere sorrow on the loss of a friend. In other words, then, Drayton's funeral elegies were personal rather than formal.

In the earliest dated one which he wrote in 1613 "Upon the Death of the Lady Penelope Clifton" (who was, as a matter of literary interest, the daughter of Sidney's "Stella"), Drayton used a very high-flown rhetoric and hyperbole. Early in the poem he included a passage which might well have come from a Jacobean tragedy:

> Walking then forth being newly up from bed,
> O Sir (quoth one) the Lady Clifton's dead.
> When, but that reason my stern rage withstood,
> My hand had sure been guilty of his blood.
> If she be so, must thy rude tongue confess it
> (Quoth I) and com'st so coldly to express it.
> Thou shouldst have given a shriek, to make me fear thee;
> That might have slain what ever had been neer thee.
> Thou shouldst have com'n like Time with thy scalp bare,
> And in thy hands thou shouldst have brought thy hair,
> Casting upon me such a dreadful look,
> As seene a spirit, or th'adst been thunder strooke,
> And gazing on me so a little space,
> Thou shouldst have shot thine eyeballs in my face,
> Then falling at my feet, thou shouldst have said,
> O she is gone, and Nature with her dead.
>
> ll. 18-32

After this wild outburst, he recalled the last time he had seen her and the grief that her loss had brought him.

In "Upon the Death of His Incomparable Friend Sir Henry Raynsford," Drayton managed a quieter tone. Sir Henry had been the husband of Anne Goodere—Idea—and Drayton had long been a close friend to the husband as well as the wife. In this elegy Drayton's verse had the manliness, strength, and direct tone of Jonson's works. The real loss he suffered comes directly to the surface of the poem. The opening of the elegy easily illustrates these qualities:

> Could there be words found to express my loss,
> There were some hope, that this my heavy cross
> Might be sustained, and that wretched I
> Might once find comfort: but to have him die
> Past all degrees that was so dear to me;
> As but comparing him with others, he
> Was such a thing, as if some Power should say
> I'le take a Man on me, to shew men the way
> What a friend should be. But words come so short
> Of him, that when I thus would him report,
> I am undone, and having nought to say,
> Mad at my self, I throw my pen away,
> And beat my breast, that here should be a woe
> So high, that words cannot attain thereto.
> 'Tis strange that I from my abundant breast,
> Who others sorrows have so well exprest:
> Yet I by this in little time am grown
> So poor, that I want to express my own.
>   I think the Fates perceiving me to bear
> My worldly crosses without wit or fear:
> Nay, with what scorn I ever have derided,
> Those plagues that for me they have oft provided,
> Drew them to counsail; nay, conspired together
> To find some one plague, that might me subvert,
> And at an instant break my stubborn heart;
> They did indeed, and only to this end
> They took from me this more than man, or friend.
>   ll. 1-28

Aside from the personal grief which moved him, Drayton also wrote of friendship and the instability of human life in this panegyric.

In the elegy "Upon the Death of Mistris Elianor Fallowfield" Drayton railed against death for its early and untimely disservice. In this short sixty-two-line poem, there is an excellent passage in which Drayton castigates Death:

> In this wide world how many thousands be,
> That having past fourscore, do call for thee.
> The wretched debtor in the Jail that lies,
> Yet cannot this his Creditor suffice,
> Doth woo thee oft with many a sigh and tear,
> Yet thou art coy, and him thou wilt not hear.

The Captive slave that tuggeth at the Oars,
And underneath the Bulls tough sinews roars,
Begs at thy hand, in lieu of all his pains,
Yet thou a niggard listenest not thereto,
With one short gasp which thou might easily do,
But thou couldst come to her ere there was need,
And even at once destroy both flower and seed.

ll. 8-22

The non-funeral poems are not what we today would consider elegies. Rather they stem from the verse epistles of Horace, and follow the pattern popularized by Ben Jonson and used by Daniel, Drayton, and Donne. These elegies have varied subjects, sometimes occasional, and sometimes topical.

Most notable are the poems addressed to Jeffreys and Reynolds. In the epistle to William Jeffreys, Drayton unleashed some of his bitterness against some of the popular poetry of the day and the low esteem in which good poetry was held at the court of King James. The quiet ending is highly effective after the railing which preceded it:

My noble friend, I would I might have quit
This age of these, and that I might have writ,
Before all other, how much the brave pen,
Had here been honoured of the English men;
Goodness and knowledge, held by them in prise,
How hateful to them Ignorance and vice,
But it falls out the contrary is true,
And so my Jeffreyes for this time adue.

ll. 111-18

The most important of Drayton's elegies is the verse epistle written to Henry Reynolds "On Poets and Poesy." In this 202-line letter Drayton traced his interest in poetry back to his very early childhood, and then he gave his critical opinions on the development of English poetry. His judgments on specific poets extended from Chaucer to his contemporaries. Many of the poets named are in sharp but brief critical vignettes which accurately picture their contributions to English letters. Especially good are the judgments on Sidney, Marlowe, and Jonson. Most of the dramatists are excluded from his poem and also all of the "cabinet poets" (those poets who failed to publish) for whom he held animosity. But what Drayton has written in this epistle stands out as clear proof of his acumen in literary criticism.

In summation, his elegies were all written in basic pentameter couplets which were not as graceful as those used in *Englands Heroicall Epistles* and did not have as high a rate of closure; but his verses did portray a rich ruggedness and directness close to the epistolary style of John Donne. The lines showed a carefully controlled firmness and strength which was the result of his high craftsmanship.

CHAPTER 6

Drayton's Poetic Theories and a Brief Survey of His Reputation

I Drayton's Poetic Theories

IT is no simple matter to piece together Drayton's theories and attitudes toward poetry; for although he wrote volume after volume of poetry over a forty-year period, and although he wrote in almost every genre popular in his day, he wrote very little prose. What little prose he did publish consisted of letters to patrons, brief prefaces to his poems, and short notes to elucidate the more obscure mythological or historical references in his poetry. No single piece of prose or poetry specifically expressed his poetic theories and attitudes. This is not to say that he did not have definite ideas and opinions on the subject of poets and poetry.

Drayton appeared on the literary scene when important changes were taking place in English poetry. The "drab" poets, with their heavy emphasis on didactic and moral poetry and their continued use of the traditional metrical forms, were being outpaced in popularity by the "golden" Petrarchists. The latter were busy with experimentation; they borrowed new metrical forms from their counterparts on the continent, and they emphasized the enjoyment of poetry. Drayton, in his early years of writing, closely allied himself with these Petrarchists.

Scattered throughout his poems are comments on the state of poetry in his time and specific passages which indicate his views on poetry. In these verses there is nothing new or startling. In them he expressed the same ideas and attitudes as the other English Petrarchists. In the expression of his ideas he was in complete agreement with Sir Philip Sidney and Edmund Spenser. He upheld the Neoplatonic concept of the "divinity" of poetry and the consequent dignity of the true poet. In company with

Sidney, Drayton was an ardent defender of what he considered the best practices in poetry.

Most of the overt comments he made on the subject of poets and poetry appeared during the first half of his writing career. And it was during this last decade of Elizabeth's reign that Drayton's poetry was most closely associated with the Petrarchists and their conventions.

In *Endimion and Phoebe* (ll. 902-14) he expressed the conventional belief in the divine origin of poetry. Such an expression was completely in accord with Neoplatonism, a common element in Petrarchan poetry in France and England. Indeed, Drayton took this particular expression directly from DuBartas' *Uranie*. And since poetry was conceived of as divine in origin, it followed that the gift of poesy must proceed from the muses themselves. *Poeta nascitur non fit.* And with this birthright, the poet became a man apart, a sort of high priest, an intermediary between the gods and man. In *The Owle* Drayton described the glory of the poet in terms such as any Neoplatonic Petrarchist might have used:

> Banisht their issue, from whose Sacred Rage,
> Flowes the full Glorie of each plenteous Age,
> Still with the Prophets challenging their parts,
> The sweet Companions of the Lib'rall Arts.
> Those rare *Promethii*, fetching fire from Heaven;
> To whom the Functions of the Gods are given,
> Raising frail dust with their redoubled flame,
> Mounted with Hymns upon the wings of Fame;
> Ordain'd by nature (Truch-men for the great)
> To fire their Noble hearts with glorious heat.
> You Sun-bred Ayerie, whose immortall Birth,
> Bears you aloft beyond the sight of Earth,
> The Heaven-tuch'd Feathers of whose sprightly wings,
> Strikes (from above) the Palace of Kings.
> By how much neerer you ascend the Sky
> Doe lessen still to every mortall Eye.
>
> ll. 667-82

The power wielded by the poet was awesome; he was able to confer immortality upon himself and the recipients of his poetic touch. In *Robert, Duke of Normandy*, Fame herself wore a breastplate on which were inscribed the words of poets (ll. 78-91). Again in Eclogue VI of Drayton's 1606 pastoral, when

Winken mourned Elphin (Sir Philip Sidney), he stressed the reward which Elphin was to receive as a poet:

> And learned Shepheard, thou to time shall live
> When their false names are utterly forgotten
> And fame to thee Eternitie shall give,
> When with their Bones their Sepulchers are rotten.
>
> ll. 101-4

And like all Petrarchists, Drayton repeated again and again in his sonnets the refrain that his poetry would confer immortality upon his mistress.

In his ideas on the purposes of poetry, Drayton echoed the expression most common in his time: the poet's aim was to please and to teach. Truth must be offered to the reader through a pleasurable medium. Thus, in *Robert, Duke of Normandy,* truth and poetry work hand in hand:

> Truth in his life, bright Poesie uphold,
> His life in truth adorning Poesie:
> Which casting life in a more purer mold,
> Preserves that life to immortalitie,
>   Both truly working, eyther glorifie;
> Truth by her power, Arts power to justifie,
> Truth in Arts roabs, adorn'd by Poesie.
>
> St. 131

Drayton's poetry had generally two broad aims which might be properly subscribed under this concept of poetry teaching through pleasure. Drayton's poetry glorified love and patriotism. In turn the love theme was divided into that of man for woman and man for man, while patriotism illuminated England's history, its land, and its language. Almost all of Drayton's poetry had one or more of these as a purpose.

The sonnets and many of the lyric odes glorify the love of man for woman; whereas many of the elegies extol friendship, or love of man for man. The pastorals, however, are frequently devoted to debates between the values of these two kinds of love. On the other hand, *Englands Heroicall Epistles* form a bridge between the glorification of love and patriotism, as they recount the loves which occurred between important figures in England's history.

The Barons Warres, The Battaile of Agincourt, The Miseries of Queene Margarite, and the various legends recall to the mind of the reader great historical events in England's past. Patriotism, as expressed in love of the homeland, is certainly one of the chief elements in *Poly-Olbion* where the poet describes the natural glories of England and Wales and recounts the historical glories attached to the land.

Although Drayton himself did no translations except in *The Harmony of the Church*, he continually defended the glory of the English language and praised those who did translate foreign works into English. Thus in his commendatory verses for Chapman's *The Georgicks of Hesiod* he praised the translator for expressing this classic in "The large dimensions of the English tongue." And in the "Epistle to Henry Reynolds" he praised those who strengthened and improved foreign works by translating them.

In many of his works Drayton offered specific suggestions as to the qualities found in good poetry. In several places he emphasized the need for decorum. To the Renaissance poet each different kind of poem had a definite set of laws which governed the content, the purpose, the tone, and the language, and which was termed decorum. Especially in his prefaces Drayton was highly explicit in giving the particular laws of the kind of poem he was then offering to the reader. Thus in his preface to his odes he carefully pointed out the different kinds of odes and what properly belonged to each type. He appealed to the classical authority of the authors of the Pindaric, Anacreontic, and Horatian odes. Then he explained why his odes could not generally be considered to follow the decorum of the Pindaric which required lofty tone and language or of the Anacreontic whose subject was solely love. Instead he chose the "mixed" or Horatian ode because "the Arguments [are] Amorous, Morall, or what else the Muse pleaseth."

He also discussed the decorum of the legend which required that some patent moralization be made for the edification and education of the reader. Thus in the brief preface to the 1619 edition of the *Legends* he wrote:

To particularize the Lawes of this Poem . . . the Principall is, that being a species of an Epick or Heroick Poem, it eminently describeth the act or acts of some one or other eminent Person. . . .

In the same passage in which he enumerated the decorum of the *Legends*, he appealed to its source, the ecclesiastical tradition of a prose life of a saint. Then he pointed out that Spenser had transferred the term to poetry.

In the preface to the *Pastorals* of 1606, he again emphasized the need for decorum as he defined his ideas on pastoral poetry. "The chiefe law of Pastorals is the same which is of all Poesie, and of all wise carriage, to wit, Decorum, and that not to be exceeded without leave or without faire warning." Touching on the sources of pastoral poetry, he briefly mentioned Theocritus and Vergil. Then he defined the requirements of the pastoral as he understood them: ordinary persons speak their simple language, yet noble ideas may well be shadowed in them.

According to Drayton, the poet must also avoid mixing genres as a breach of decorum. He accused himself of this fault in his "Epistle to Master William Jeffreys." He tells that he is writing an elegy in which he bewails the baseness of the times, but he has lost sight of his original purpose and has let a strong note of satire capture the spirit of his verse. He admits that this mixture was a failure on his part.

One of the most important passages in his works which indicate his views on the writing of poetry occurred in the third nimphall of *The Muses Elizium*. In this poem Drayton gave four examples of poetry, three he considered to be poor, and one he considered to be a model of well-written poetry. The first poem is a "madding" bout between two swains in which they recite wildly and extravagantly. There is no real sense to what they are saying; there is only excessive emotion and feeling expressed. In the second song two nymphs engage in a similar bout. But here the verse lacks emotion and intensity. The verses consist of a series of clichés and tortured rhymes. The third song has emotion, description, and a thought; but it lacks order in that the verses have no real beginning, middle, or end. Finally, a hymn is sung to the Muses in which all of the proper elements of poetry are carefully balanced. By contrast to the imperfect examples preceding it, the hymn becomes a commentary on poetry. It condemns the swains' song which lacked intellectual control over the emotions expressed; it censures the song of the nymphs for its lack of that inspiration which gives originality to a poem; and finally it dismisses the third song for its omission of a rational frame. These four songs give in an indirect manner Drayton's ideas on the importance of proper balance of thought and emotion, and the control of both within a poem.

Most of Drayton's views on poetry were completely in keeping with those of his early Petrarchan associates, and his early work shows that he faithfully applied these tenets to his own writing. Indeed, a summing up of his early work might be this: he applied artificial emotions and conventions to an accepted poetic form. In other words his early poetry applied to a world of conventions, a non-realistic world. It became in a sense a poetry of escapism, as *Arcadia* was a prose escape form.

However, to Drayton's credit, he did not remain in this artificial world of set conventions and conceits. During the reign of James I, Drayton's poetry turned toward a real world. His lyrics began to treat of real human attitudes and problems. Thus in the sonnets, "How many paltry, foolish painted things," "In pride of Wit, when high desire of Fame," "Since ther's no helpe, come let us kiss and part," he treats of conditions and attitudes which belong not to an accepted convention but to real life. Such odes as "The Rivall," "The Cryer," and "The Heart" continue the perusal of the real human heart. In this move from the stylized conventions and attitudes of the Petrarchists, Drayton was not denying his views on poetry; he was merely expanding them. He had realized and practiced the truth that if good poetry can be written within an artificial framework bound by stylized convention, better and more lasting poems can be written about the real world where the subjects and attitudes expressed can find echoes in the mind and hearts of the reader.

Drayton retained the craftsmanship he learned in the Petrarchan school; he merely broadened his intellectual and emotional horizons in the vastness of the living world. It was this expansion of his viewpoint which gave his later lyric poetry its lasting richness.

Another quality he acquired in the seventeenth century was his dramatic expression of reality. As a former playwright he was able to dramatize his lyrics so that they presented a truly visual scene to the reader. "The Cryer" and "How many paltry, foolish painted things" express such dramatic scenes as the speakers evoke in the imagination, a vignette which so easily happens in life.

Two kinds of poets annoyed Drayton throughout his entire literary career. Among the first were those poets who refused to publish their work for submission to the general public. In his elegy "On Poets and Poesy" after he had discussed his contemporaries he remarked:

> For such whose poems, be they nere so rare,
> In Private chambers, that incloistered are,
> And by transcription daintily must go;
> As though the world unworthy were to know,
> Their rich composures, let those men keep
> These wondrous reliques in their judgement deep,
> And cry them up so, let such Peeces be
> Spoke of by those that shall come after me,
> I passe not for them.
>
> ll. 185-94

He attacked poets who offered their talents to the highest bidder in *The Owle* (ll. 685-94), and he also condemned those who were either incompetent (*The Moon-calfe*, ll. 391-98) in their use of the English language or a "ryming Slave" ("A Skeltoniad," ll. 15-28). Drayton was grievously disappointed during the reign of James I at the lack of royal patronage on behalf of what Drayton himself considered to be good poetry.

Drayton's final attitude toward poetry and his own aims in writing poetry during his last years can be summed up in his own words in this passage from the twenty-first song of *Poly-Olbion.* In it is seen the view not of the Petrarchist of the Golden Age of Elizabeth but the mature and polished forerunner of the Neoclassicist:

> Give me those Lines (whose touch the skilfull ear to please)
> That gliding flow in state, like swelling *Euprates,*
> In which things naturall be, and not in falsely wrong:
> The Sounds are fine and smooth, the Sense is full and strong,
> Not bumbasted with words, vain ticklish ears to feed;
> But such as may content the perfect man to read.
> What is of Paynters said, is of true Poets rife,
> That he which doth express things neerest to the life,
> Doth touch the very poynt, nor needs he add thereto:
> For that the utmost is, that Art doth strive to do.
>
> ll. 184-93

II   A Brief Survey of Drayton's Reputation

With the chief exception of the poetry of Shakespeare and
Spenser, most of the works of the Elizabethan poets disappeared
from popular view from the latter seventeenth century until the
beginning of the twentieth century. However, Drayton's poetry
did not share this temporary oblivion. Indeed, readers continued
to enjoy much of his delightful poetry.

Edmund Spenser was one of the first poets of major rank to
pay tribute to Drayton.[1] In *Colin Clouts Come Home Againe* he
listed twelve contemporary poets who were popular in 1595. The
last of the group was Aetion, also referred to as Rowland. To the
Elizabethan reader Rowland, the chief shepherd in *Idea, The
Shepheards Garland* was as familiar as Colin in *The Shepherds
Calendar.* For this reason the majority of recent Drayton scholars
have identified Aetion with Drayton. Of Aetion Spenser wrote:

> A gentler shepherd may no where be found:
> Whose muse full of high thoughts invention,
> Doth like himself heroically sound.
>
> ll. 447-49

As Drayton continued to write and publish his poetry, his
popularity increased. In 1600 Robert Allot compiled a dictionary
of quotations from poetry popular at that time. About sixty
poets were represented in the 2350 quotations in *Englands Parnassus.* Spenser was most frequently represented with 389 passages, 298 of which were from *The Faerie Queene.* In second
place, but far ahead of his nearest rival, was Drayton with 225
quotations from all of his then published works.[2] Following him
in a close grouping were William Warner's *Albions England,*
Thomas Lodge, Samuel Daniel, and Harington's translation of
Orlando Furioso. Although not conclusive, such a listing indicates a popular ranking of the poets of the day.

Ben Jonson knew Drayton, although they were not close
friends. Most of their relationships were at second hand through
their mutual friend, Drummond of Hawthornden. At the turn of
the century there was some bitterness between the two (Jonson
and Drayton), as the Countess of Bedford had withdrawn her
patronage from Drayton and then used it to advance Jonson.

Because of this Drayton had made him the butt of satire in two of his poems. Jonson returned in kind with a sly dig in *The Returne from Parnassus*, part II:

> Draytons sweet muse is like a sanguine dy,
> Able to ravish the rash gazers eye.
> However, he wants one true note of a poet of our
> times and that is this, he cannot swagger it
> well in a tavern nor domineer in a hot house.
>
> Act I, sc. ii

In 1627 Jonson wrote a lengthy commendatory poem for *The Battaile of Agincourt*. Jonson's poem was called "The Vision of Ben. Jonson, on the Muses of his Friend M. Drayton." The first fifteen lines admit that the world might not have considered them friends, because they had not yet exchanged commendatory verses. Then Jonson summarizes Drayton's major works. He finally ends with a brief expression of hopeful friendship. In reading this poem, one finds a real and basic admiration for Drayton's poetry. However, Jonson, the satirist, could not resist overdoing the admiration in spots so that the effect cannot help bringing a smile to the lips of the reader. Thus he praises *Poly-Olbion*:

> . . . Thou hast made thy way
> And flight about the Ile, well near, by this,
> In thy admired Periegeis,
> Or universal circumduction
> Of all that read thy Poly-Olbion.
> That read it? that are ravish'd! such was I
> with every song, I swear, and so would dye:
>
> ll. 48-54

After complaining that *The Miseries of Queene Margarite* caused him to weep so much that he was unable to read the lines, he turned to *Nimphidia* with undiluted praise:

> But then refreshed with thy Fairy Court,
> I looke on Cynthia and Sirenas sport
> As, on two flow'ry carpets, that did rise,
> And with their grassy green restor'd mine eyes.
>
> ll. 79-82

William Browne and George Wither were two younger poets who looked upon Drayton as an admired survivor of an earlier golden age. Browne again and again made flattering allusions to Drayton in the first two books of *Britannia's Pastorals*. And in the concluding lines of a commendatory poem for the second part of *Poly-Olbion* he called upon time to bear Drayton's muse to Ovid, Vergil and Homer. "They would confess, that never happier Pen,/Sung of his Loves, his Country, and the Men." Wither championed Drayton fourteen years after the latter's death in *The Great Assizes Holden in Parnassus*. When Drayton's ability as a poet was challenged with reference to *Poly-Olbion* as a "crude embryon of wit," Apollo gave a long and spirited eulogy in praise of his high poetic talents and achievements. The "defense of Drayton is stronger than is made on behalf of any of his fellow 'jurours'—Wither, Carew, May, Davenant, Sylvester, Sandys, Beaumont, Fletcher, Heywood, Shakespeare, and Massinger."[3]

After Drayton's death and the passing on of his contemporaries, his works did not disappear from public sight. Milton read and appreciated Drayton's works. The editors of the Columbia Edition of Milton's works found fifteen passages which contained echoes or imitations from Drayton's poems. One of these was in *Lycidas*; one, in *Paradise Lost*; three, in *Il Penseroso*; and seven, in *Comus*. And the parallels were found in a highly varied selection of Drayton's writings: two in *The Barons Warres*; one in *Eclogs*; three in *The Muses Elizium*; one in *Nimphidia*; one in *The Owle*; six in *Poly-Olbion*; and one in "Upon the death of three sons of Lord Sheffield."

In 1675 Milton's nephew, Edward Phillips, wrote a pertinent comment on Drayton in his *Theatrum Poetarum*. He suggested that Drayton was not much inferior to either Sidney or Spenser, although he was somewhat antiquated, especially in regard to *Poly-Olbion*. But he added that *Englands Heroicall Epistles*, the fairy poetry, and the pastorals were still being read and enjoyed.

The eighteenth century saw no slackening in Drayton's popularity. However, with the change of tastes, the emphasis on Drayton's poetry turned to *Englands Heroicall Epistles* and *Poly-Olbion*. In his study of *Elizabethan Poetry in the Eighteenth Century*, Earl R. Wasserman points out that the epistles "were second only to Spenser's *Fairy Queene* in their popularity and influence in the eighteenth century."[4] This interest was probably a result of their form as couplets and their orthodoxy as a descendant of the classic of Ovid. This is not to say that the Augustans did not find fault with the uneven numbers they saw in his poems. On the contrary, they rewrote, improved, and imitated these poems, bringing them to the taste of this age of enlightenment.

Aside from the *Epistles* and the fairy poetry, *Poly-Olbion* had a vogue all its own during the eighteenth century. Excerpts from Drayton's magnum opus were frequently reprinted, and many of the topographical poets of the age leaned heavily upon this work as a primary source.[5] The antiquaries also took a great interest in *Poly-Olbion*. They frequently used it in their efforts to apply scholarship to works of the Renaissance. For their editions of Shakespeare, Spenser, and Milton, they made use of the multitude of facts in which *Poly-Olbion* abounded.[6]

Of the poets and critics in the eighteenth century, Pope considered Drayton to be but a mediocre poet; Oliver Goldsmith and the dilettante Horace Walpole spoke slightingly of his ability. On the other hand James Kirkpatrick, Thomas Warton, John Campbell, and Dr. Johnson had high praise for Drayton's works.

In the nineteenth century Drayton's popularity continued unabated. Charles Lamb, Thomas Campbell, and William Hazlitt spoke highly of his poetic skill. The latter described *Poly-Olbion* as a work of "great length and unabated vigor,"[7] although he found it monotonous. However, Lamb found in the same work "life and passion beyond the dreams of old mythology."[8]

Robert Southey, Isaac Disraeli, Richard LeGalliene, Edmund Gosse, George Saintsbury, and A. H. Bullen were all in agreement as to the importance of Drayton as a Renaissance poet. In almost every case they echoed the criticism which had preceded them. However, with new editions of Drayton's original poetry published at mid-century they were able to appreciate his work in its original form uncorrected by the Augustans. In general they considered him a poet who sometimes had difficulty with expression, but who had originality of conception and force and variety of style.

We have barely touched upon the many people who read and delighted in Drayton's poetry in the three hundred and thirty odd years since his death. But from this we can indeed see that Drayton's literary reputation did not sink into oblivion after the Commonwealth period as happened to so many of the Elizabethan poets. Drayton, unlike Donne or Daniel, did not have to wait to be rediscovered in the twentieth century. Even as poetic tastes changed over the passing years, poets and critics always found in his poetry a quiet and endless enjoyment.

CHAPTER 7

General Conclusions

MANY of the critics of Michael Drayton have considered him a poet who remained an Elizabethan throughout his entire poetic career. The analysis of his poetical theories as he stated them in his poetry seems to bear out this assumption. However, an analysis of the entire body of his poetry indicates that this is neither an adequate nor an accurate judgment. In an examination of the individual poems it is easy to see that Drayton moved with the changing times in his poetic techniques. The early poems clearly show correspondences with the other Elizabethan poets. Thus in his early pastorals, as *Idea, The Shepheards Garland,* there are the same poetic techniques which Spenser used. In *Matilda* we see the influence of Daniel; in *Endimion and Phoebe* we discover that of Marlowe; and in the first editions of the sonnets there are close relationships with Daniel, Spenser, and Sidney.

However, as time progressed and poetic tastes and patterns changed, Drayton's poetry also changed. Thus, in the later sonnets such as "Methinks I see some crooked Mimic jeer," and "Since ther's no helpe, come let us kiss and part," we can easily see how Drayton has progressed beyond the styles and motifs of his early masters. The metaphysical conceits in such later odes as "The Heart" and "The Cryer" closely resemble the techniques utilized by Donne and the Metaphysical school. The tone of the elegies is similar to those of Ben Jonson. "Nimphidia" and the eighth nimphall of *The Muses Elizium* foreshadow the lightness and delicateness of Herrick's fairy poetry, and the "Quest of Cynthia" has the simplicity and sweetness of Carew. Finally, the ode "To His Rivall" has the light cynicism of the Cavalier poets in their approach to love. Drayton was not merely an Elizabethan poet; he was one whose poetic abilities could and did grow with the passage of time. The comparison of his pastorals of 1593 and 1606 with those of 1627 and 1630 easily proves this point.

Another charge frequently leveled at Drayton was that he was merely an imitator, and not an original poet. This too becomes patently absurd when the entire canon of his works has been examined. Like most young writers, Drayton did lean heavily upon his sources in the early years of his poetic apprenticeship. But this was not frowned upon in the Renaissance; an author was fully permitted to take the work of others as long as he reworked and "improved" it. Thus without embarrassment on his behalf, we can admit that in the first edition of *Ideas Mirrour* many of the sonnets frequently had close correspondences with those of Daniel, Sidney, and Spenser, and that *Matilda* had close relationships with *The Complaint of Rosamund*. But again as time passed, more and more of Drayton's sonnets and his other poems became increasingly original in style, content, and tone.

Far from being a mere imitator, Drayton was an inveterate experimenter both in genre and in prosody. *Englands Heroicall Epistles, Nimphidia, The Muses Elizium* and his odes were all original contributions he made to the respective genres, and differed completely from the poetic practices which preceded him. He combined the historical and the love poem in *Englands Heroicall Epistles*; he evolved the pastoral into a new form with the *Nimphidia* and *The Muses Elizium*, and he established the Horatian ode as a firm genre in English literature.

Also in the realm of prosody he introduced new variants into the English meters commonly used by his fellow poets. In *Englands Heroicall Epistles* he gave smoothness and form to the heroic couplet. More than any of his predecessors he moved toward the closed form of the couplet. He prepared the way for Dryden and Pope with his use of antithesis and apothegms in the couplets. Other innovations were his introduction of many new meters and stanzaic forms from the French lyricists in his odes. Another variant was the extension of the tail rhyme in *Nymphidia*, where, by adding a foot to each line, he eliminated the burlesque quality, but kept the rollicking, quickly moving action. Even in *Poly-Olbion* he gave the despised hexameter new life. With a careful use of a varied caesura and a distribution of end-stopped and run-on lines, the long measure became to a certain extent regenerated.

Another mark of credit should go to Drayton for his continual revisions. He was his own sharpest critic, and he continuously tried to improve his previously published verses, seeking to make them more nearly correct, smoother, and more enjoyable for the reader. In his earliest work the lines were encrusted with the heavy ornamentation and tortured metaphors which were the mark of the Petrarchan English poet. As he revised his older poems and wrote new ones, he gradually dropped these techniques and moved toward lines which gave the reader real and dramatic images in their place. In his later work he restored the balance between the ideas he was expressing and the techniques used to express them. In the 1590's, Drayton overcharged his poems with figures which inflated an artificial emotion beyond the value of the thoughts which were stated. However, as he revised, he began to balance the value of the emotion with that of the concept expressed.

Closely allied to this development in his revisions was Drayton's struggle with rhetoric and syntax. As time progressed he solved part of his rhetorical problem by decreasing his use of adjectives and adverbs and placing heavier stress on action verbs. But the difficulty with syntax was harder to overcome. In the earliest poems his sentence structure was exceedingly complicated and frequently twisted tortuously to fit into his metrical line and make his rhyme. But as his skill improved over the years, he gradually corrected and simplified his syntax, especially in his lyric poetry. By using direct speech, he was able to eliminate many of the subordinate clauses which had caused the early poetry to be somewhat ponderous and stilted.

Since Drayton had spent four years in which he had earned his living as a playwright (1597-1601), it might be presumed that writing for the stage helped him in a great measure to overcome this difficulty. As a support for this hypothesis, it can be noted that the actual simplification of the syntax in his poetry began in those poems which were published after he finished his playwriting. By the 1620's he had this problem solved in his lyrics and his pastoral poems; but he still had it, though to a much lesser extent, in his late historical poems.

In the twentieth century it is an established habit to attempt to label a man and his work. Thus some of the critics speak of Drayton as primarily a pastoralist, an historical poet, a topographical poet, or a lyricist. However, in his case such labeling is misleading and erroneous. Drayton was engaged in a wide variety of literary activities. He was at once a sonneteer, pastoralist, satirist, historian, antiquarian, scholar, and lyricist in many modes. No one label can possibly describe him with any degree of justice. Because of his diversity and the high level of quality which generally marks his poetry, it seems proper that the name of Drayton might be advanced for the title of "the complete Renaissance Poet."

T. S. Eliot once remarked that to be a great poet one had to write in a variety of genres with high competence, with some poems of unsurpassed excellence. Michael Drayton's work fits these requirements. He was a highly skilled craftsman who wrote poems of extreme competence in almost every genre available in his day. Of the kinds of poetry popular during his career, he missed none. He translated, wrote minor epics, pastorals, histories, and lyrics of every type. Even in the religious poems which are the least successful in his canon, there is a general level of competence and even some brilliant passages. None of his works can be described as technically incompetent. He was well aware of the differing requirements needed for each genre, and he fulfilled those requirements with care.

There is no doubt that in some of his poems he rose to the highest poetic levels. Several of his sonnets in the 1619 edition, *The Quest of Cynthia, The Muses Elizium, Nimphidia,* "To the Virginian Voyage," "The Ballad of Agincourt," and the elegy to Henry Reynolds "On Poets and Poesy" are unsurpassed in their literary modes. In addition, ever since he first began writing, Drayton's poetry has never dropped from the public view. Even though poetic tastes changed radically, there has always been a Drayton following who has appreciated his particular genius.

Notes and References

Chapter One

1. Two sonnet sequences were published in 1592; four in 1593; three in 1594; five in 1595; three in 1596; and one each in 1598, 1599, 1604, and 1609.
2. Charlotte C. Stopes, *Shakespeare's Warwickshire Contemporaries* (1907), p. 191.
3. Sir Sidney Lee, *Elizabethan Sonnets* (1904), p. lxxxviii.
4. Stopes, *op. cit.*, p. 191.
5. J. W. Hebel, *et al.*, *The Works of Michael Drayton*, 5 vols. (1931-41), V, 15. Hereafter, this edition is referred to as *Works*.
6. Leah Jonas, *The Divine Science* (1940), p. 59.
7. The original Renaissance spelling has been arbitrarily modified in some instances to aid the modern reader.
8. Oliver Elton, *Michael Drayton: A Critical Study* (1905), p. 54. Some of the other sequences which are referred to throughout this chapter are Samuel Daniel's *Delia*, Sir Philip Sidney's *Astrophel and Stella*, Edmund Spenser's *Amoretti*, Thomas Lodge's *Phillis*, Henry Constable's *Diana*, Thomas Watson's *Hekatompathia* and *Tears of Fancie*, Barnaby Barne's *Parthenophil and Parthenope*, Bartholomew Griffin's *Fidessa*, William Smith's *Chloris*, and Giles Fletcher's *Licia*.
9. Lisle Cecil John, *The Elizabethan Sonnet Sequence* (1936), pp. 93-95; *Works* V, 17.
10. John, *op. cit.*, pp. 130-32.
11. *Ibid.*, pp. 87-90.
12. Cyril Brett, "Introduction," *Minor Poems of Michael Drayton* (1907), p. xxi.
13. *Works* V, 14.
14. Robert Hillyer, "The Drayton Sonnets," *The Freeman*, VI, 489.
15. Lu Emily Pearson, *Elizabethan Love Conventions* (1933), p. 193.
16. T. W. H. Crosland, *The English Sonnet* (1917), p. 161.
17. John, *op. cit.*, pp. 90-122.
18. C. S. Lewis, *English Literature in the Sixteenth Century* (1954), p. 496.
19. A tabular analysis of the six major editions of *Idea*. The six columns represent the numbering in each major edition of Drayton's Sonnet sequence. In order the columns are from the 1594, 1599, 1600, 1602, 1605, and 1619 editions. (T: To the Reader; D: Dedicatory;

P: Prefatory Sonnet; E: with *Englands Heroicall Epistles*). In the 1600 ed. Sonnets 30, 31, 36, and 37 are misnumbered respectively 40, 41, 46, and 47. In the 1605 ed. three sonnets were numbered 61, and two were numbered 62.

x	1	1	1	P	E	The world's fair Rose, and Henries frosty fire
x	2	2	2	T	T	Into these Loves, who but for Passion looks
x	3	3	3	T	x	Many there be excelling in this kind
11	4	4	4	1	x	Thine Eyes taught me the Alphabet of love
x	x	x	x	x	1	Like an adventurous Sea-farer am I
x	5	5	5	2	2	My heart was slain, and none but you and I
10	6	6	6	3	3	Taking my pen, with words to cast my woe
9	7	7	7	4	x	Beauty sometime in all her glory crowned
x	x	65	66	63	4	Bright star of beauty, on whose eyelids sit
x	8	8	8	5	5	Nothing but No and I, and I and No
x	9	9	9	6	x	Love once would dance within my Mistres eye
x	x	x	x	x	6	How many paltry, foolish painted things
x	10	10	10	7	7	Love, in a humour, play'd the Prodigall
x	11	11	11	8	x	Phoebe look down, and here behold in me
x	x	x	x	x	8	There's nothing grieves me, but that Age should haste
x	x	12	12	9	9	As other Men, as I my self do Muse
x	12	13	13	10	10	To nothing fitter can I Thee compare
x	13	14	14	11	11	You not alone, when You are still alone
x	14	15	15	12	12	That learned Father, which so firmly proves
21	15	16	16	13	13	Letters and lines we are soon defaced
36	16	x	x	x	x	Sweet sleep so arm'd with Beauties arrows darting
x	x	17	17	14	14	If he, from Heav'n that filched that living fire
14	17	18	18	15	x	Viewing the glass of my youth's miseries
x	x	x	x	x	15	Since to obtain thee, nothing me will sted
6	18	19	19	16	16	In one whole world is but one Phoenix found
7	19	20	20	17	17	Stay speedy time, behold before thou pass
8	20	21	21	18	18	To this our world, to Learning and to Heaven
x	21	22	22	19	19	You cannot love, my prettie heart, and why
x	22	23	23	20	20	An evil spirit your beautie haunts me still
x	23	24	24	21	x	Thou which do'st guide this little world of love
x	x	x	x	x	21	A witless Gallant, a young wench that woo'd
x	x	25	25	22	22	With Fools and children good Discretion bears
x	24	26	26	23	23	Love banish'd Heav'n, in Earth was held in scorne
x	x	27	27	24	24	I hear some say, this man is not in love

x	25	28	28	25	25	O, why should Nature niggardly restrain
37	26	29	29	26	26	I ever love, where never Hope appears
x	27	30	30	27	x	I gave my fayth to Love, Love his to me
x	x	x	x	x	27	Is not Love here, an 'tis in other climes
x	x	31	31	28	28	To such as say, Thy love I over-prize
32	28	32	32	x	x	Those tears which quench my Hope, still kindle my desire
x	29	33	33	29	29	When conquering Love did first my Heart assayle
x	30	34	34	30	30	Those Priests which first the Vestall Fire begun
x	31	35	35	31	31	Me thinks I see some crooked Mimick jeer
24	32	36	36	32	32	Our Flouds-Queen Thames, for Ships and Swans is crowned
33	33	37	37	33	33	While yet mine Eyes do surfet with Delight
x	34	38	38	34	34	Marvell not, Love, though I thy pow'r admire
12	35	39	39	35	35	Some Atheist or vile Infidell in Love
20	36	40	40	36	x	Reading sometyme, my sorrows to beguile
x	x	x	x	x	36	Thou purblind Boy, since thou hast been so slack
x	x	x	41	37	37	Dear, why should you command me to my rest
31	37	41	42	38	38	Sitting alone, Love bids me go and write
18	38	42	43	39	39	Some, when in Ryme, they of their Loves do tell
44	39	43	44	40	40	My Heart the Anvil, where my thoughts do beat
43	40	44	45	41	41	Why do I speak of Joy, or write of Love
27	41	45	46	x	x	My Love makes hot the fire whose heat is spent
28	42	46	47	42	42	Some wits there be which like my Method well
x	x	x	x	43	43	Why should your fair Eyes with such sov'raine grace
x	43	47	48	44	44	While thus my pen seeks to eternize thee
x	44	48	49	45	45	Muses which sadly sit about my Chayre
x	x	x	x	46	46	Plaine-path'd Experience, th'unlearneds guide
x	x	x	x	47	47	In pride of Wit, when high desire of Fame
26	45	49	50	48	x	Cupid, dumb Idoll, peevish Saint of Love
x	x	x	x	x	48	Cupid, I hate thee, which I'd have thee know
x	46	50	51	49	49	Thou Leaden Brain, which censur'st what I write

x	x	x	x	50	50	As in some countries, far remote from hence
x	x	x	x	51	51	Calling to mind since first my Love begun
22	47	51	52	52	x	My hart imprisoned in a hopeless Ile
x	x	x	x	x	52	What do'st thou mean to Cheat me of my Heart
13	48	52	53	53	53	Cleer Ankor, on whose Silver-sanded shore
1	49	53	54	54	54	Read here (sweet Mayd) the storie of my woe
2	50	54	55	55	55	My fayre, if thou wilt register my love
3	51	55	56	56	56	My thoughts bred up with Eagle-birds of love
x	x	x	x	57	57	You best discern'd of my Minds inward Eyes
4	52	56	57	x	x	My fayre, had I not erst adorned my Lute
x	x	x	x	58	58	In former times, such as had store of Coyn
x	x	57	58	59	59	As Love and I, late harboured in one Inn
49	53	58	59	60	60	Define my weal and tell the joys of heaven
x	x	x	x	x	61	Since ther's no help, come let us kiss and part
50	54	59	60	61	62	When first I ended, then I first began
x	55	60	61	62	63	Truce, gentle Love, a parley now I crave
x	56	61	62	x	x	Eyes with your tears, blind if you be
x	x	62	63	61	x	Not thy grave Counsells, nor thy Subjects love
x	57	63	64	61	x	Great Ladie, essence of my cheefest good
x	58	64	65	62	x	Madam: my words cannot express my mind
D	59	66	67	64	x	Vouchsafe to grace these rude, unpolish'd rymes

(The following sonnets appeared only in the 1594 edition.)

5	Since holy Vestall laws have been neglected
15	Now Love, if thou wilt prove a conqueror
16	Vertues Idea in Virginitie
17	If ever wonder could report a wonder
19	If those ten Regions registered by Fame
23	Wonder of Heaven, glass of divinitie
25	The glorious sun went blushing to his bed
29	O eyes, behold your happy Hesperus
30	Three sorts of Serpents do resemble thee
34	My fayre, looke from those turrets of thine eyes
35	See chaste Diana, where my harmless hart
38	If chaste and pure devotion of my youth
39	Die, die, my soul, and never taste of joy
40	O thou unkindest fayr, most fayrest she
41	Rare of-spring of my thoughts, my deerest Love

42 Plac'd in the forlorn hope of all despayr
45 Black pitchy Night, companion of my woe
46 Sweet secrecie, what tongue can tell thy worth
47 The golden sun upon his fiery wheels
48 Who list to praise the days of delicious lyght
51 Go you my lines, Embassadors of love

20. Pearson, *op. cit.*, p. 196.
21. *Works* V, 56.
22. Pearson, *op. cit.*, pp. 196, 206.
23. *Works* V, 16.
24. George Saintsbury, *A History of Elizabethan Literature* (1887), p. 114.
25. Mario Praz, "Michael Drayton," *English Studies*, XXVIII (1947), 101.

Chapter Two

1. Other pastorals which were popular during these days were: *The Arraignment of Paris* by George Peele in 1584; *An Eclogue Congratulatorie* by Robert of Essex in 1589; Thomas Watson's *Amyntas* translated by Abraham Fraunce in 1587; Sir Philip Sidney and the Countess of Pembroke's *Arcadia* in 1593; *Rosylynde* by Thomas Lodge in 1590; Thomas Greene's *Mourning Garment* and Thomas Watson's elegiac eclogue on Thomas Walsingham the same year; *The Affectionate Shepherd* by Richard Barnfield in 1594; and various pastoral pieces in *England's Helicon* in 1600. After the turn of the century the pastoral vogue continued with the Countess of Pembroke's "A Dialogue between Two Shepherds" and William Basse's *Three Pastorall Elegies of Anader, Anetor, and Muridella* in 1602; the latter author also issued *Passionate Shepherd* and *Fantastics* in 1604; Henry Chettle printed his *England's Mourning Garment* in 1603. A decade later William Browne's first book of *Britannia's Pastorals* was published, and then a year later his *The Shepheards Pipe* appeared. Drummond of Hawthornden issued *Teares on the Death of Moliades* in 1613 and two years afterward George Wither printed *The Shepheards Hunting*.

2. A comparison of the order of the eclogues in the two editions can be seen here. Note that references to the first edition are in Latin numerals and the 1606 references are in Arabic figures.

1. (I)   Rowland alone.
2. (II)   Motto and Winken: Debate of youth and age on love.
3. (III) Perkin and Rowland: Panegyric to Beta.
4. (VIII) Motto and Gorbo: Golden age and "Dowsabell."
5. (V)   Motto and Rowland: Panegyric to Idea.

6. (IV)   Gorbo and Winken: Dirge for Elphin.
7. (VII)   Batte and Borrill: Debate.
8. (VI)   Perkin and Gorbo: Praise of several women.
9. —   Full Chorus: The Shepherd's Holiday
10. (IX)   Rowland alone.

Ray L. Heffner, Jr., *Michael Drayton as Pastoral Poet* (1953), p. 89.

3. Heffner, *op. cit.*, pp. 120-22.

4. Floris Delattre, *English Fairy Poetry from the Origins to the Seventeenth Century* (1912), pp. 181-84.

Chapter Three

1. The idea of using historical literature to express erotic love was very popular during the later Elizabethan and early Jacobean periods. In 1563 Thomas Churchyard's *Shore's Wife* appeared in the *Mirrour for Magistrates*. In *Albion's England* Warner linked up many of the romantic incidents which dotted that country's history. In 1592 Samuel Daniel published *The Complaint of Rosamund* and William Wyrley's *True Use of Armorie* contained two long complaints against fortune by fourteenth-century heroes.

The next year Thomas Lodge issued *The Complaint of Elstred* and Anthony Chute retold the story of Mistress Shore in *Beawtie Dishonored*. And finally Giles Fletcher, the elder, published *The Rising to the Crowne of Richard III* in which he derided the tender emotions of both Rosamund and Elstred.

2. Homer Nearing, Jr., *English Historical Poetry, 1599-1641* (1945), p. 24.

3. *Works* V, 32.

4. Glenn P. Haskell, *Drayton's Secondary Modes* (1936), p. 193.

5. Louis R. Zocca, *Elizabethan Narrative Poetry* (1950), p. 79n. Zocca here states that *Cromwell* was included in the 1587 edition of *The Mirrour for Magistrates*. I can find no evidence which could possibly support such an assertion.

6. *Works* V, 167-72.

7. *Works* V, 64.

8. Specific Catalogs are given in the following passages in the poem: 265f., 361f., 505f., 633f., 737f., 1097f., 1137f., 1457f., and 2193f.; *Works*, III, 15-63.

9. Nearing, *op. cit.*, p. 178.

10. W. J. Courthope, *A History of English Poetry* (1903), III, 42.

11. Hallet Smith, *Elizabethan Poetry* (1952), p. 129; Robert Hillyer, *loc. cit.*; Praz, *loc. cit.*

12. Louis B. Wright, *Middle-Class Culture in Elizabethan England* (1935), p. 332.

Chapter Four

1. Hilda Taylor, *Topographical Poetry in England in the Renaissance* (1926), pp. 19-20; Robert Aubin, *Topographical Poetry in XVIII-Century England* (1936), Chapter I. These two works begin with surveys which show the incidental use of topographical verse from the Classical through the Medieval period.

2. Taylor, *op. cit.*, pp. 81-123. She discusses Tudor poetry and the various masques which contain topographical elements as well as the personifications of geographical entities.

3. Some of the passages occur in the following: II:60; II:137; V:240; VII:256; XII:520; XIII:19; XIII:249; XIV:55; XVII:381; XIX:41; XXII:1611; XXIII:11.

4. Thomas P. Harrison, *They Tell of Birds: Chaucer, Spenser, Milton, Drayton* (1956), p. 135.

5. Bernard Newdigate, *Michael Drayton and His Circle* (1941), p. 168.

6. Lewis F. Ball, "Minor English Renaissance Epics," *ELH*, I, (1934), 63.

7. Robert Lathrop Sharp, *From Donne to Dryden: The Revolt against Metaphysical Poetry* (1940), p. 99.

8. Ball, *op. cit.*, pp. 84-99.

9. Aubin, *op. cit.*, p. 17.

10. *Ibid.*, pp. 21-23.

Chapter Five

1. Haskell, *op. cit.*, p. 80.

2. *Works* V, 2.

3. Haskell, *op. cit.*, p. 249; *Works* V, 175-81; Heffner, *op. cit.*, pp. 119-20.

4. Thomas P. Harrison, *op. cit.*, pp. 111-12. Also in this context Elton thought that the crane might be Drayton, but Hebel disagreed. Jenkins offered the conjecture, which found no supporters, that the Jay represented John Donne. Kathleen Tillotson suggested that the oak incident referred to the fall of the Earl of Essex. Hebel further thought that the vulture represented Lord Cecil and the turtle dove was Arabella Stuart whose marriage to William Seymour had been opposed by Cecil. Elton, *op. cit.*, p. 98; *Works* V, 179; Raymond Jenkins, "Drayton's Relation to the School of Donne as Revealed in *The Shepheards Sirena*," *PMLA*, XXXVIII, 576-77; Kathleen Tillotson, "Drayton and Richard II," *Review of English Studies* XV, 179.

5. *Works* V, 175.

6. In *The English Ode to 1660* Samuel Shafer pointed out that Drayton was the first English poet to correlate the English ode with its Classical sources, and to restrict the applicability of the term in accordance with its Classical framework (pp. 83-84). Drayton's performance with the ode, according to Shafer, "rises far above that of any of his predecessors, and marks the real beginning of the odes as a separable lyric 'kind' in our poetry (p. 91). Both Shafer (p. 89) and Sir Sidney Lee in *The French Renaissance in England* (239f.) believed that Drayton had borrowed directly from the French for his odes. Thus they pointed out that "To Himselfe, and the Harpe" was modeled on Ronsard's "A sa Lyre," and that "To the new yeere" resembled DuBellay's "Du Primier Jour de l'An." However, Hebel and Tillotson (*Works* V, 144-45) in their discussion of this matter, while admitting the many benefits Drayton drew from the French, maintained that Drayton's odes were completely his own and in no sense translations or paraphrases.

7. *Works* V, 281.

Chapter Six

1. Some other contemporaries who praised Drayton in their works were Nicholas Baxter, Richard Barnfield, Thomas Lodge, Edward Guilpin, Charles Fitz-Jeffries, Robert Tofte, John Weever, Sir William Alexander, John Beaumont, Thomas Greene, and Joshua Sylvester.

2. The Drayton quotations in *Englands Parnassus* were from the following poems: *Idea*, 1599–1; *Endimion and Phoebe*–18; *Mortimeriados*–58; *Piers Gaveston*–30; *Matilda*–38; *Robert, Duke of Normandy*–13; and *Englands Heroicall Epistles*–67.

3. Newdigate, *op. cit.*, pp. 195-96.

4. Earl R. Wasserman, *Elizabethan Poetry in the Eighteenth Century* (1947), p. 47.

5. Selected passages from *Poly-Olbion* were printed in Nathaniel Salmon's *Antiquities of Surrey, Universal Magazine* in 1747, 1763, 1784, 1796, *Gentleman's Magazine* in 1750, 1760, 1766, Charles Deering's *Nottinghamia Vetus et Nova* in 1751, Robert Dodsley's *Miscellany* in 1758, William Maitland's *History and Survey of London* in 1756, John Dyer's *The Fleece* in 1761, *Kentish Traveller's Companion* in 1779, and Joseph Budworth's *Fortnight Ramble to the Lakes* in 1796.

6. *Poly-Olbion* was used in the notes for the following works: Francis Peck's *New Memoirs of the Life and Poetical Works of Mr. John Milton*, 1740; Zachary Scott's *Hudibras*, and *Critical, Historical,*

and Explanatory Notes on Shakespeare; and John Upton's *Critical Observations on Shakespeare* and the 1758 edition of Spenser's *Faerie Queene.*

7. William Hazlitt, *Complete Works,* ed. P. P. Howe, 21 vols. (1930-34), VI, 311.

8. Charles and Mary Lamb, *Works,* ed. E. V. Lucas, 5 vols. (1903), I, 45; IV, 46.

Selected Bibliography

PRIMARY SOURCES

BRETT, CYRIL, ed. *Minor Poems of Michael Drayton*. Oxford: Clarendon Press, 1907.

BULLEN, A. H., ed. *Selections from the Poems of Michael Drayton*. Chilworth, England: Unwin Bros., 1883.

BUXTON, JOHN, ed. *Poems of Michael Drayton*. 2 vols. Cambridge: Harvard University Press, 1953. This is the second best collection presently available of Drayton's poetry. Although this work does not contain the complete canon, it does have an excellent selection with a rather good preface.

COLLIER, J. PAYNE, ed. *Poems of Michael Drayton*. London: J. B. Nicholas and Sons, 1856.

HEBEL, J. W. *et al.*, eds. *The Complete Works of Michael Drayton*. 5 vols. Oxford: Shakespeare Head Press, 1931-41. This is the definitive Drayton edition. The first four volumes contain all of his poems in one or more major editions, and the fifth volume contains all of the many variants of the poems as Drayton revised them. From this volume one can reconstruct any poem as it appeared in any of Drayton's many editions.

————. ed. *Endimion and Phoebe: Ideas Latmus by Michael Drayton*. Stratford-upon-Avon: Shakespeare Head Press, 1925. Another one of Hebel's brilliant Drayton re-creations. This work is especially good for the excellent critical essay which precedes the poem.

SECONDARY SOURCES

AUBIN, ROBERT A. *Topographical Poetry in XVIII Century England*. New York: Modern Language Association, 1936. Influence of *Poly-Olbion* on eighteenth-century topographical literature.

BALL, LEWIS F. "Minor English Renaissance Epics." *ELH, Journal of English Literary History*. I (1934), 63-89. The classification of *Poly-Olbion* as an epic.

BERTHELOT, JOSEPH A. *A Handbook of the Poetical Works of Michael Drayton*. Unpublished Ph. D. Thesis, University of Denver, 1962. The study is basically the source book for this edition.

BULLEN, A. H. *Elizabethans*. London: Chapman & Hall, Ltd., 1925. A short but excellent commentary on the sonnet sequence.

BUSH, DOUGLAS. *English Literature in the Early Seventeenth Century 1600-1660*. New York: Oxford University Press, 1952. A standard work in the *Oxford History of English Literature* Series.

————. *Mythology and the Renaissance Tradition in English Poetry*. Minneapolis: University of Minnesota Press, 1932. A good discussion of the role of mythology in Tudor and Jacobean poetry.

CAMPBELL, LILY BESS, ed. *The Mirror for Magistrates*. New York: Barnes & Noble, 1960. An excellent preface which gives the rationale of the Mirrour stories.

————. *Tudor Conceptions of History and Tragedy in "A Mirror for Magistrates."* Berkeley: University of California Press, 1936. A valuable aid in understanding Drayton's "Legends."

CORY, HERBERT E. "The Golden Age of the Spenserian Pastoral." *PMLA*, XXV (1910), 241-67. A comparative view of Drayton and Spenser in the pastoral mode.

COURTHOPE, W. J. *A History of English Poetry*. London: Macmillan, 1903. Vol. III, Chapter III. A representative nineteenth-century view of Drayton.

COWLEY, R. R. "Drayton and the Voyagers." *PMLA*, XXXVIII (1923), 530-56. An excellent discussion of the source and inspiration for "To the Virginian Voyage."

————. "Drayton's Use of Welsh History," *Studies in Philology*, XXII (1925), 234-55. A study of some of the sources for the *Poly-Olbion*.

CROSLAND, T. W. H. *The English Sonnet*. London: Martin Secker, 1917. An excellent view of the many sonnet sequences of the English Renaissance.

DELATTRE, FLORIS. *English Fairy Poetry from the Origins to the 17th Century*. London: H. Froude, 1912. A scholarly analysis of the influence of fairy poetry upon Drayton's later work.

DRAPER, JOHN W. *The Funeral Elegy and the Rise of English Romanticism*. New York: New York University Press, 1929. Credits Drayton as being a major influence in bringing the funeral elegy into popularity in English verse.

ELTON, OLIVER. *An Introduction to Michael Drayton*. Manchester: J. E. Cornish, 1895. The first full-length study of Drayton's complete works.

————. *Michael Drayton: A Critical Study*. London: A. Constable, 1905. An amplification of the earlier work with a more critical but still highly sympathetic point of view.

Englands Parnassus comp. by Edward Allot, 1600, ed. by Charles Crawford. Oxford: Clarendon Press, 1913. A collection of quotations made during Drayton's early period, which illustrates the popularity of his poetry.

FINNEY, CLAUDE L. "Drayton's *Endimion and Phoebe* and Keats' *Endymion*," *PMLA*, XXXIX (1924), 805-13. An excellent article showing Drayton's influence on John Keats.

GOURVITCH, IVAN. "Drayton's Debt to Geoffrey of Monmouth," *Review of English Studies*, IV (1928), 394-403. Another source study of the *Poly-Olbion*.

————. "A Note on Drayton and Philemon Holland." *Modern Language Review*, XXV (1930), 332-36. A comparative study of historical materials for *Poly-Olbion*.

————. "The Welsh Element in the Poly-Olbion," *Review of English Studies*, IV (1928), 69-77. Further notes on sources of *Poly-Olbion*.

GREG, W. W. *Pastoral Poetry and Pastoral Drama*. London: A. H. Bullen, 1906. An excellent standard work on the role of the pastoral, especially in the Renaissance.

HARRISON, THOMAS P. *They Tell of Birds: Chaucer, Spenser, Milton, Drayton*. Austin: University of Texas Press, 1956. A highly competent analysis of Drayton's use of birds, both descriptive and satiric.

HASKELL, GLENN PERCIVAL. *Drayton's Secondary Modes, A Critical Study*. Unpublished Ph. D. Thesis: University of Illinois, 1936. A superior and well-documented study of the odes, elegies, satires, and other minor works. Each mode is carefully placed within its literary and historical context.

HEBEL, J. W. *vide* Drayton.

————. "Drayton and Shakespeare," *Modern Language Notes*, XL (1926), 248-50. A short note on the alleged collaboration of Drayton and Shakespeare.

————. "Drayton's Sirena," *PMLA*, XXXIX (1924), 816-36. A possible identification of whom "Sirena" represents.

HEFFNER, RAY L., JR., *Michael Drayton as Pastoral Poet*. Unpublished Ph. D. Thesis: Yale University, 1953. This scholarly work carefully analyzes Drayton's pastorals from the historical and literary view. Excellent documentation and bibliography.

HELTZEL, VIRGIL B. *Fair Rosamond*. Evanston: Northwestern University Press, 1947. A study of the poem which heavily influenced Drayton's "Matilda."

HILLYER, ROBERT. "The Drayton Sonnets," *The Freeman*, VI (January 31, 1923), 488-89. A listing and analysis of a few of Drayton's best sonnets.

HOLMES, ELIZABETH. *Aspects of Elizabethan Imagery.* Oxford: Black-well, 1929. A highly informative study with many excellent examples of Petrarchan types.

HULL, VERNAM E. *The English and Welsh Topographical Sources of Drayton's Polyolbion.* Unpublished Ph. D. Thesis: Harvard University, 1926. The major study on the geographical nature of Drayton's long work.

JENKINS, RAYMOND. "Drayton's Relation to the School of Donne as Revealed in *The Shepheards Sirena,*" *PMLA,* XXXVIII (1923), 557-87. A search in Drayton's work for references to Donne and his friends.

————. "The Sources of Drayton's *Battaile of Agincourt,*" *PMLA,* XLI (1926), 280-93. A good analysis of the sources.

JOHN, LISLE CECIL. *The Elizabethan Sonnet Sequences.* New York: Columbia University Press, 1936. A sensitive and critical view of the sonnet sequence.

JONAS, LEAH. *The Divine Science.* New York: Columbia University Press, 1940. Contains an excellent study on the role of the poet in literature.

LEE, SIR SIDNEY. *Elizabethan Sonnets.* London: A. Constable, 1904. A thorough but mediocre study of the sonnet sequence.

————. *The French Renaissance in England.* New York: Scribners, 1910. Very valuable in comparing Drayton's use of the mono-strophic ode with that of the French poets.

LEVER, J. W. *The Elizabethan Love Sonnet.* London: Macmillan, 1956. Another superb study of the sonnet sequence. Sensitive and informative.

LEWIS, C. S. *English Literature in the Sixteenth Century.* New York: Oxford University Press, 1954. A must for the overview of Tudor English Literature.

LONG, EDGAR. "Drayton's Eighth Nymphall," *Studies in Philology,* XIII (1916), 180-83. A short analysis of part of "The Muses Elizium."

NEARING, HOMER, J. *English Historical Poetry, 1599-1641.* Philadelphia: University of Pennsylvania, 1945. Excellent for understanding how Drayton's historical poetry fits into its literary context.

NEWDIGATE, BERNARD. *Michael Drayton and His Circle.* Oxford: Shakespeare Head Press, 1941. A careful study from literary sources of Drayton's life and friends.

NOYES, RUSSELL. *Michael Drayton's Literary Vogue Since 1631.* Bloomington: University of Indiana Press, 1935. An historical view of Drayton's popularity since his death.

Selected Bibliography

PEARSON, LU EMILY. *Elizabethan Love Conventions.* Berkeley: University of California Press, 1933. An excellent study, especially of the Petrarchan conceit in late Tudor poetry.

PRAZ, MARIO. "Michael Drayton," *English Studies,* XXVIII (1947), 97-107. An appreciation primarily of the sonnets.

ROLLINS, HYDER EDWARD. *England's Helicon 1600, 1614.* 2 vols. Cambridge: Harvard University Press, 1935. Contains several of the "Songs" from Drayton's early pastorals.

ST. CLAIR, F. Y. "Drayton's First Revision of His Sonnets," *Studies in Philology,* XXXVI (1939), 40-59. A brief analysis of the changes in the sonnets from 1594 to 1599.

SAINTSBURY, GEORGE. *A History of Elizabethan Literature.* London: Macmillan, 1887. A standard in the field.

————. *A History of English Prosody.* London: Macmillan, 1923. II, 97-104. A discussion of Drayton's prosodical contributions to English poetry.

SHAFER, SAMUEL R. *The English Ode to 1660.* Princeton: Princeton University Press, 1918. Places Drayton in perspective relative to the development of the English ode.

SHARP, ROBERT LATHROP. *From Donne to Dryden: The Revolt against Metaphysical Poetry.* Chapel Hill: University of North Carolina Press, 1940. Discusses in part Drayton's later poetry.

SHORT, R. W. "Ben Jonson in Drayton's Poems," *Review of English Studies,* XVI (1940), 149-58.

————. "Jonson's Sanguine Rival," *Review of English Studies,* XV (1939), 315-19. Both articles attempt to identify real people masked in Drayton's poetry.

SIMPSON, PERCY. A reply to Short's articles *Review of English Studies,* XVI (1940), 149-58. A disagreement with Short's identifications.

SMITH, HALLET. *Elizabethan Poetry.* Cambridge: Harvard University Press, 1952. An excellent survey.

STOPES, CHARLOTTE CARMICHAEL. *Shakespeare's Warwickshire Contemporaries.* Stratford-upon-Avon: Shakespeare Head Press, 1907. Briefly places Drayton within the context of his contemporaries in his home county.

TANNENBAUM, SAMUEL A. *Michael Drayton: A Concise Bibliography.* New York: Samuel Tannenbaum, 1941. An excellent and comprehensive bibliography of Drayton editions and criticism from the poet's time to 1941.

TATLOCK, JOHN S. P. "Origin of the Closed Couplet in English," *The Nation,* XCVIII (April 9, 1914), 390. A discussion of Drayton's place in the development of the heroic couplet.

TAYLOR, DICK B., JR. "Drayton and the Countess of Bedford," *Studies in Philology*, XLIX (1952), 214-28. A study of the relationships between Drayton and his patroness.

TAYLOR, HILDA. *Topographical Poetry in England in the Renaissance.* Chicago: University of Chicago, 1926. An excellent work which shows the influence and popularity of *Poly-Olbion.*

TILLOTSON, GEOFFREY. "Contemporary Praise of *Poly-Olbion,*" *Review of English Studies*, XVI (1940), 181-83. The reaction of the Jacobeans to the publication of Drayton's topographical poem.

TILLOTSON, KATHLEEN. "Drayton and Richard II: 1597-1600," *Review of English Studies*, XV (1939), 172-79. Suggested relationships during his dramatic period to *Richard II.*

————. "Drayton, Browne, and Wither," *London Times Literary Supplement*, November 27, 1937, 911. A brief commentary on Drayton's influence on two other pastoralists.

————. "The Language of Drayton's *Shepheards Garland.*" *Review of English Studies*, XIII (1937), 272-81. A comparison of the use of archaic and rustic language in the Drayton and Spenser pastorals.

————. Reply to Short's articles *Review of English Studies*, XVI (1940), 305-6. Disagreement with Short's identifications.

WASSERMAN, EARL R. *Elizabethan Poetry in the Eighteenth Century.* Urbana: University of Illinois Press, 1947. Good commentary on the rewriting of some of Drayton's poetry and its popularity in the eighteenth century.

WHITAKER, LEMUEL. "Michael Drayton as a Dramatist," *PMLA*, XVIII (1903), 378-409. An excellent study of Drayton's little-known dramatic work.

————. "The Sonnets of Michael Drayton," *Modern Philology*, I (1904), 563-67. A brief appreciation of a few of the sonnets.

WIATT, WILLIAM HAUTE. *Englands Heroicall Epistles: A Critical Study.* Chapel Hill, N. C.: University of North Carolina Press, 1955. The comprehensive analysis of the "Epistles."

WINTERS, YVOR. "The Sixteenth Century Lyric in England." *Poetry.* LIII (1939), 258-72, 320-35; LIV (1939), 35-51. One of the best of the discussions of the Elizabethan lyric from the viewpoint of the Petrarchan versus the Native schools.

ZOCCA, LOUIS R. *Elizabethan Narrative Poetry.* New Brunswick: Rutgers University Press, 1950. A good commentary on Drayton's "legends" and other historical poems.

Index

Index

Index

ABOUT THE AUTHOR

Joseph A. Berthelot is currently an Associate Professor of English at the United States Air Force Academy, where he has been teaching since 1958. Professor Berthelot's long career as a teacher began after receiving his B.A. from Assumption College, Ontario, Canada. He served in the United States Air Force, where he attained the rank of Major, and, following his return to civilian life, earned the M.A. from Texas Western College and the Ph.D. from the University of Denver. Since 1964, he has been a contributing editor to the Annual Bibliography of English Language and Literature of the Modern Humanities Research Association. At the present time, he is working on two books. One is a study of the Renaissance pre-novelist, Thomas Deloney. The other, which stems from his interest in Renaissance Spanish mystical literature, is an analysis of the works of the contemporary American, Thomas Merton, with special emphasis upon the influence in his work of the writings of St. Teresa of Avila and St. John of the Cross.